NEW VANGUARD 225

REPUBLICAN ROMAN WARSHIPS 509–27 BC

RAFFAELE D'AMATO   ILLUSTRATED BY GIUSEPPE RAVA

First published in Great Britain in 2015 by Osprey Publishing,
PO Box 883, Oxford, OX1 9PL, UK
PO Box 3985, New York, NY 10185-3985, USA
E-mail: info@ospreypublishing.com

Osprey Publishing, part of Bloomsbury Publishing Plc

© 2015 Osprey Publishing Ltd.

All rights reserved. Apart from any fair dealing for the purpose of private study, research, criticism or review, as permitted under the Copyright, Designs and Patents Act, 1988, no part of this publication may be reproduced, stored in a retrieval system, or transmitted in any form or by any means, electronic, electrical, chemical, mechanical, optical, photocopying, recording or otherwise, without the prior written permission of the copyright owner. Enquiries should be addressed to the Publishers.

A CIP catalogue record for this book is available from the British Library

Print ISBN: 978 1 4728 0827 1
PDF ebook ISBN: 978 1 4728 0828 8
ePub ebook ISBN: 978 1 4728 0829 5

Index by Alan Rutter
Typeset in Sabon and Myriad Pro
Originated by PDQ Media, Bungay, UK
Printed in China through Worldprint Ltd

15 16 17 18 19   10 9 8 7 6 5 4 3 2 1

Osprey Publishing/Shire Publications supports the Woodland Trust, the UK's leading woodland conservation charity. Between 2014 and 2018 our donations are being spent on their Centenary Woods project in the UK.

www.ospreypublishing.com

Title page image: A naval scene from the fresco of the Villa of Farnesina. (Roma, Museo Nazionale Romano, photo D. Carro, courtesy of the museum)

DEDICATION
To Domenico Carro, the man who introduced me to my love for the Roman navy.

ACKNOWLEDGEMENTS

A great number of people, museums, and institutions have contributed to this book. The help of Professor Livio Zerbini of Ferrara University in obtaining from museums and institutions permission to see and photograph material has been as always invaluable, and in particular for the precious photos of the National Archaeologic Museum of Aquileia, for which I am also indebted to Dr. Luigi Fozzati, Soprintendente per i beni archeologici del Friuli Venezia Giulia..

Very special thanks must be given to Admiral Domenico Carro, who shared with me his precious photographic collection on monuments related to the Roman Navy, enriching the book with wonderful illustrations. A second very special acknowledgement is due to the Soprintendente del Mare of Regione Sicilia, Sebastiano Tusa, and to the RPM Nautical Foundation. The wonderful material related to the *rostra* and helmets of the Aegates Islands and the *rostrum* of Acqualatroni are published for the first time here thanks to their kindness.

The material in this book from the Musei Capitolini, the Antiquarium of the Palatino and the Museo Nazionale di Palazzo Massimo is thanks to D.ssa Marina Mattei, curator of the Musei Capitolini and director of the Excavations of the Area Sacra di Largo Argentina. The finds of Comacchio have been published only thanks to the help of Dr. Fede Berti of the Museo Archeologico di Ferrara, to whom I would like to express all my gratitude for her assistance.

I would like to express my great thanks to Professor Gabriella Pantò, director of the Museum of Antiquities of Torino, for her helpful assistance during my research visit and for her kind permission to publish the necessary material; to Dr. Patrizia Petitti of the Museum of Antiquities of Torino, for her hard work; and to Dr. Mario Epifani, director of the Royal Armoury (Armeria Reale) in Torino, for kind permission to publish the photo of the fragment of *proembolion* preserved there. Another important acknowledgment should be given to the Museum Guarnacci of Volterra, and in particular to my late friend Gabriele Cateni. A further thanks is due to the Museum Lapidarium of Narbonne.

Special thanks must also be given for the ever-precious assistance of Dr. Andrea Salimbeti and Dr. Massimo Bizzarri in collecting photos, searching the sources, preparing drawings, patiently assisting in my various travels and many other numerous activities. Last but not least, I am deeply grateful to my dear friend and illustrator Giuseppe Rava for his splendid, dramatic and dynamic illustrations that have brought to life the world of the early Roman navy.

GLOSSARY

Epotis, επωτις:	thick beam at the forward end of an outrigger or oarbox, cathead
Foredeck:	the deck forward of the *epotis*, and aft of the stempost
Louvre:	protected ventilation course
Hortator:	man who directed the rowers
Navis, Naves:	ship, ships
Parasimon, παρασημον:	panel on each side of the bow of a warship facing half-front containing symbols or figures illustrating the ship's name
Parexeiresia, παρεξειρεσια:	outriggers, auxiliary fittings for the oars, small arches on the external structure of the hull on which the oars of the *traniti* found their foothold
Parodos, παροδος:	gangway
Proembolion:	fore ram or subsidiary ram that projects forward above the waterline ram, whose purpose is to prevent entanglement or damage to the ship's superstructure at the bow, during ramstrikes
Stempost, *prora*:	the curved timber rising from the keel in the bow and culminating in an ornament or figure-head
Stolos:	ornament of the prow
Thalamian, Talamiti:	the lowermost oarsmen on a three-level warship
Wale:	assemblage end to end of thick and broad planks along a ship's side, worked into the hull planking
Zygian, Zigiti:	upper oars level, uppermost oarsmen on a three-level warship

CONTENTS

INTRODUCTION — 4

HISTORICAL BACKGROUND — 4
- The origin of the Roman navy
- The first known Roman warships
- The second Sea Treaty
- The growth of Roman sea power

ROMAN SHIPS AND FLEETS — 9
- Structure and construction
- Early Roman warships: undecked *aphraktai* and other *pentéconterae*
- The *trireme*
- The *quadrireme*
- The *quinquereme*
- The bigger *polyremes*
- The *Lembos biremes* and the *liburnae*
- The *oneraria*
- Other ships

DECORATION AND EQUIPMENT — 19
- Colour and decoration

ARMAMENT AND TACTICS — 22
- The ram
- The 'raven'
- Turrets
- Fighting on the sea: Roman naval tactics

ROWING A ROMAN WARSHIP — 27
- Rower disposition
- Keeping rhythm

CAMPAIGNS — 31
- The First Punic War
- The Second Punic War
- Operations in Greece
- Pompey and the Cicilian Pirates
- Caesar in Gaul
- The naval wars of Octavianus and Agrippa

SELECT BILLIOGRAPHY — 46

INDEX — 48

REPUBLICAN ROMAN WARSHIPS 509–27 BC

INTRODUCTION

Republican Rome's navy originated from the clash of the 3rd century BC Mediterranean superpowers, when Carthage was the master of the western Mediterranean at sea, and the young Roman *Res Publica* had already conquered the Italian Peninsula. On the sea Carthage seemed invincible, and at the beginning of the First Punic War the Roman fleet was mostly only provided with small undecked units, called *aphracktai*, of Etruscan typology. The Romans at first copied and then surpassed the better technology of their Carthaginian enemies, using innovative military technology and tactics such as the *corvus*, or 'raven'. The Romans' admirable capacity for organization, combined with their practical common sense, more than made up for their deficiencies in naval warfare and tactics and allowed them to destroy Carthaginian maritime power forever, thus opening the way for Rome's relentless rise and her dominance of the Mediterranean basin for the next seven centuries.

The legacy of Rome's naval power is significant. The Roman shipyards developed some of the basilar techniques of modern naval architecture, such as the technique of building from the keel upwards. Numerous generations of sailors coming from the coasts and harbours of Italy were a continuous presence in the Roman fleets in these early centuries of Rome's navy. Rome's navy assured the continuity of its maritime supplies, and that the republic could control the Mediterranean Sea and push their sails to the borders of the known world, or even beyond. This, the first of a series of New Vanguard books examining Rome's warships, covers the period from the birth of Rome's navy to the beginning of the Imperial period.

HISTORICAL BACKGROUND

The origin of the Roman navy
From the earliest times, the Romans regarded the sea as having a divine character. In legend, after his escape from Troy the mythical hero Aineias wandered the Mediterranean before eventually arriving with his fleet on the coast of Latium. Here he built Lavinium (Pratica di Mare); his descendants included Romulus and Remus, the twins who would found Rome, and the *Julia Gens*, the family of Julius Caesar. So, since the beginning the naval element was linked with the holy in Rome's tradition: to escape the

destruction at the hands of the Latins, the Trojan fleet was transformed by the gods from wooden ships into beautiful sea nymphs.

Since the age of the early kings, the Romans had increasingly used the river Tiber as a natural link between Rome and the sea, until in 640–616 BC, under King Ancus Marcius, the Romans created their first sea harbour. According to Livy (I,33), after the Romans conquered the Etruscan city of Veii, they founded there the new city of Ostia. Ostia was fortified, and the king likewise made the channel clear for tall ships and for sailors seeking a livelihood on the sea (Ennius, *Fragm*. 146–147).

In 509 BC, on the eve of the Consular Age, Carthage, the dominant maritime power in the western Mediterranean, concluded a Sea Treaty with Rome. Throughout the 6th century Rome was still an Etruscan city and shared in the Etruscan confederacy's maritime power in the Tyrrhenian Sea. Rome, a novice in maritime affairs, considered, like Athens, the pursuit of sea power to be a means of acquiring power generally, and of course as a means of safeguarding the food supply of the growing *Urbs*. Unlike Athens, where the people participated in the decisions of the community according to the census, the common Roman people who formed the crews of the early ships had no influence on this policy, which was decided firstly by the kings and later by the magistrates.

The Romans, of course, by signing a treaty with Carthage, clearly already had some maritime power and an interest in expanding trade in overseas regions (perhaps as supposed from Polybius, using warships). As regards, in particular, the coastal security against possible threats coming from the sea, it should be noted that one of the last initiatives of Tarquin the Proud (the last king of Rome) before losing his throne, was to send Roman colonists to Circeum so that this area would become one of the maritime ramparts of the city. It can also be supposed that since Carthage accepted the Sea Treaty, Roman naval power was not insignificant even at this time. The treaty was renewed five times.

Detail of a sailor's equipment on an Etruscan Urn representing Odysseus and the Sirens, 3rd century BC. (Volterra, Museum Guarnacci, author's photo, courtesy of the museum)

With the growth of the Roman population, the supply of the *Urbs* should have been primarily secured by sea. This matter soon became the object of a constant concern of the Roman government. According to Livy, Rome bought wheat at Cuma (near Naples), but the Roman ships were detained by the tyrant Aristodemus, heir of Tarquin the Proud, in compensation for the seizure of the former king's property.

The first known Roman warships

The first mention of Roman warships is from 394 BC. In this year, after the victories of Marcus Furius Camillus over

Faleria and Veii, the Senate sent a warship to Delphi, in Greece, to deliver a pot of gold to be offered to Apollo. Not far from the Straits of Messina, the ship was forced inside the piratical port of Lipari. In this city the practice was to divide any authorized seizures among the people. But the chief magistrate that year was a certain Timasiteus, who, full of respect for their status as ambassadors and for Apollo, welcomed the ambassadors as guests, sent them to Delphi under naval escort, and allowed them back to Rome unharmed. It is clear that even the powerful Lipari also feared a Roman naval reaction. In this period Rome also concluded a Naval Treaty with the Tarentine, under which the latter protested in 282 BC when a flotilla of Roman warships entered the Tarents' harbour. With this treaty, which was never renewed, the Romans acknowledged to the Tarentine the right of the exclusive use of the Gulf north of Cape Lacino, (namely Cape Colonna). It is not clear, however, which bond had been imposed, by reciprocity, on the ships of Tarent.

The first mention of a Roman maritime war is from 349 BC. The *Consul* Lucius Furius Camillus, son of the great statesman Marcus, had been entrusted with command of the war against the Gauls, and in this year he gave orders to the *Praetor* to defend the entire coastline of Latium and keep away a small Greek fleet that was ravaging the coast. The following year, having defeated the Gauls, the *Consul* received orders from the Senate to assume command of the sea war (*bellum maritimum*), and joined his troops with those of the *Praetor*. Camillus had no opportunity to force action against these Greeks; they were mediocre fighters on land, as the Romans were at sea at this time, and thus they kept away from shore. Without water supplies and everything else essential to life, they left Italy. To which Greek people that fleet belonged we cannot establish with certainty, although Admiral Carro believes that they were *Siceliotes*.

The second Sea Treaty
From the second Sea Treaty between Rome and Carthage, signed in 348 BC, we have the proof that the Romans used their warships for piracy. The text, reported by Polybius (3,24) translates as follows:

> There shall be friendship between the Romans and their allies, and the Carthaginians, Tyrians, and township of Utica, on these terms: The Romans shall not maraud, nor traffic, nor found a city east of the Fair Promontory, Mastia, Tarseium. If the Carthaginians take any city in Latium which is not subject to Rome, they may keep the prisoners and the goods, but shall deliver up the town. If the Carthaginians take any folk, between whom and Rome a peace has been made in writing, though they be not subject to them, they shall not bring them into any harbours of the Romans; if such a one be so brought ashore, and any Roman lay claim to him, he shall be released. In like manner shall the Romans be bound towards the Carthaginians... In Sardinia and Libya no Roman shall traffic nor found a city; he shall do no more than take in provisions and refit his ship. If a storm drive him upon those coasts, he shall depart within five days. In the Carthaginian province of Sicily and in Carthage he may transact business and sell whatsoever it is lawful for a citizen to do. In like manner also may a Carthaginian at Rome.

This new naval treaty shows a higher level of consideration and heightened caution of the Carthaginians against the Roman naval presence. It has more explicit constraints on expansion (in the Carthaginian possessions in Sardinia and North Africa), behaviour (no piracy in certain areas), and geographic restrictions on all Roman activity in the western Mediterranean, (in the Carthaginian areas of Spain south of Mastia). The Carthaginians emphasised the fact of their entire possession of Libya and Sardinia, and prohibited any Roman attempt to land there at all; on the other hand, in the case of Sicily, they clearly distinguished their own province in it. So, too, the Carthaginians were obliged to respect Ardea, Antium, Circeii, and Terracina – all of which are on the seaboard of Latium, to which alone the treaty refers. Thus, here we have the possibility of a list of centres where the Latin warships were located.

Etrusco-Roman ship and sailors of the Punic Wars on an Etruscan Urn representing Odysseus and the Syrens, 3rd century BC. (Volterra, Museum Guarnacci, author's photo, courtesy of the museum)

The growth of Roman sea power

Shortly afterwards, Alexander of Epirus attempted a landing against the Lucans, in Bruttium (nowadays the Italian province of Basilicata), who prevented him fighting the Romans. This proved Italy's maritime vulnerability on those coasts not yet controlled by Rome. It was an event which would contribute to the Romans' growing awareness of the need to expand their capabilities in naval surveillance and defence. However, during the landing of Alexander of Epirus, the Romans were also confronted with the more pressing need to bring under their control the Latin cities that had opened hostilities, including in 340 BC the naval raids carried out by the Antiates against the territories of Ostia.

Two years later, in 338 BC, the consuls Lucius Furius Camillus and Caius Menius had subdued all Latium, and in Antium a new Roman colony was created. The Antiates' warships were carried away and they were banished from the sea. Some of the Antiates' ships were brought inside the Roman naval docks (*navalia*), some burned, and some of the ships' prows were taken to embellish the grandstand being built in the Forum, which took the name of *rostra* (Livy, III,1; Plinius, XXXIV,11,20). The ships taken from Antium formed the first nucleus of a small effective navy, compact but consistent with Rome's still-limited role as a regional power. The Romans interpreted this *imperium* also in terms of sea power, by foreclosing the sea to the Antiates, so as not to have any interference from other local fleets. During the wars of 343 BC, to protect the cities of the Campania against the Samnites, the Romans formed an alliance with Paleopolis-Neapolis, which with its ships became the first powerful *socius navalis* (naval allies) of the Roman fleet.

The Samnite wars allowed the Romans to complete and consolidate their control over the coastal strip, where the more significant maritime cities of the Tyrrhenian coast were centred. The final outcome was that Rome took

Roman warship, from Etruscan Urn of 1st century BC. Note the stern tower with its pitched top, similar to those represented in the *denarii* of the *Fonteia Gens*. (Volterra, Museo Guarnacci, author's photo)

greater interest in and responsibility towards the Adriatic and Ionian shores, thus enhancing their navy and leaving only the Greeks of Tarentum with the sea power to oppose Rome's acquisition of full hegemony over the Italian Peninsula. In 312 BC two further military powers (*imperia*) were given to the *plebs* (the popular class) – the appointment of 16 military tribunes, and the appointment of the so-called *duoviri navales classis ornandae reficiendaeque causa*, a post responsible for fitting out and repairing the fleet (Livy, IX,30,4). It is clear that the fleet had already assumed the dimensions that required the establishment of a special magistrate of the State. According to Livy (XL,18,7, XLI,1,2-3) each of the *duoviri* commanded a squadron of ten ships.

The activity of the Roman fleet at that time was merely patrolling the coasts and raiding the shores – more or less a kind of piracy. It is enough to remember a curious little episode which occurred in 311 BC. Publius Cornelius, to whom the Senate had entrusted the surveillance of the coast towards Campania, landed in Pompeii and his allied sailors plundered the territory of Nocera. Hastily raiding an area from where they could safely return to the ships, they were attracted by the prospect of further booty and penetrated deeper into the country, awakening their enemies. While they were dispersed through the countryside, no one moved to meet them, although it would have been easy to kill them all. However, when they returned in groups, without precautions, the farmers surprised them not far from the ships and killed many, retaking the booty. Leaving aside the grotesque aspects of this farmer battle, certainly due to the fact that these 'allies' did not yet have the combat experience of the Romans, it is significant to note that the Roman fleet had already been mandated by the Senate to delegate tasks of naval surveillance to auxiliary naval forces.

Of interest is the fact that this activity took place just off Campania, clearly demonstrating that Rome, as soon as she was able to claim the alliance of all the maritime cities of that region, wanted to take their place in exercising sea power in that area. In 306 BC the Carthaginian Sea Treaty was renewed for the third time (Livy, IX,43,26), protecting Africa and Sardinia as areas of exclusive influence of the Carthaginians. Nothing was said, however, about Corsica, already the subject of Roman attention. In 307 BC the Romans arrived with 25 ships, investigating the possibility of founding a colony, but the island proved to be a wild place, thick with trees that prevented the Romans from landing. The idea of building a colony there was abandoned for the time being.

In 292 BC sources (Valerius Maximus I,8,2; Ovidius 15, 622–744; Livy X,47) mention a Roman warship, specifically indicated as a *trireme* (a ship with three banks of oars), which was sent on an official visit to Greece for religious reasons: because the city was plagued by an epidemic disease the Senate sent ambassadors to bring an image of Aesculapius (a god of medicine

Fragment of Roman warship, 1st century BC. Note the bronze prow, fastened to the hull by means of big bronze rivets, the decorated *proembolion* ending with a ram head, the apotropaic eye on the portside, and the triton used as name-device (*parasimon*). (Antiquarium of Palatino, photo D. Carro, courtesy of the museum)

with a serpent-entwined staff), from the port of Epidaurus to Rome on a Roman *trireme*. On their arrival in the waters of the Tiber, the serpent was said to have 'jumped from the Latin ship' onto Tiber Island, where a temple to Aesculapius was built in honour of the miracle. The Isola Tiberina was shaped like a ship, and today the shape is still visible. The study of its original form has allowed scholars to understand the possible shape of the earlier Roman *triremes*. The monument was probably rebuilt in the 1st century BC with precious marble travertine, sperona and peperibo, and the original *trireme* took the shape of a flagship of 100–50 BC, probably a consular 'Five' or a 'Six' *polyreme*.

ROMAN SHIPS AND FLEETS

Structure and construction

The Roman navy, especially in the historical period of the Punic Wars and of the conquest of the Mediterranean, reached a level of fleet size, complexity and technological sophistication unsurpassed until the 19th century. We should also remember that in the more complex examples of Hellenistic naval engineering during this age of great cultural and scientific flowering in the Mediterranean, ships with a large number of rowers and a complex multi-deck rowing system were commonplace, and this system was adopted and improved by the Romans. Only around 1800, with the first appearance of hulls of iron-reinforced wood, can we consider the technological leadership of the ancients over.

Until the First Punic War, Carthage was the preeminent naval power in the western Mediterranean. But Roman naval technology underwent a transformation during this war, when a Carthaginian ship was captured and copied piece by piece, and Rome ordered a rapid building of 160 new advanced warships to this design. Some scholars, analysing Polybius's account of this incident, considered it doubtful that a people devoid of naval tradition would have been able to 'copy' a captured ship. But

Roman *assis* of 2nd century BC, showing a *longa navis rostrata* with anchor. (Medagliere Capitolino di Roma, photo D. Carro, courtesy of the Musei Capitolini)

Patera from Cales with representations of *triremes* or *quinqueremes*, 3rd to 2nd century BC, signed by the potter Canoleios. The *patera* was used to pour wine during the sacrifices. The presence of warships denotes a probable destination of the cult of protective deities of the fleet (*Lari marini*) and navigation. All the ships, aft of the eye and beneath the ventilation course, have a deep oar panel, showing on its lateral face three courses of oarports arranged quincunx fashion. (Napoli, Museo Archeologico Nazionale, photo D. Carro, courtesy of the museum)

Naval battle scene from the crater of Aristhonos, 7th century BC, (Musei Capitolini, Roma, author's photo, courtesy of the museum)

there is nothing strange in this, for the Romans were not alone in the Mediterranean.

It is enough to note that all the technical words used for the earlier Roman ships were of Greek origin, such as *scaplius*, *navis*, *nauta*, and *carina*. The ships could be built from freshly cut wood, and the Greek carpenters who served the Romans knew where to find it, how to choose it, cut it and shape it. They were qualified shipwrights. Who better than the Greeks to build a fleet for their Roman allies and teach them how to employ it at sea? If the Roman fleet was built in only two months as Polybius suggests, it was obviously because it was either built in the Greek arsenals of Magna Graecia or by Greeks in Roman arsenals.

If we accept that neither the Romans nor their allies in Campania, who were used to building *pentaconterae* and *triremes*, knew the technique of building *quinqueremes*, it is likely that, to save time, they began construction of simpler ships with a single rank of oars, each operated by five men.

Regarding the wood used and construction techniques of Roman ships, we know most about the *onerariae* cargo ships; no remains of a Roman warship of the Consular Age have yet been discovered and identified, except the bronze parts. However, the recently found shipwreck of Antikythera, an *oneraria* ship of 87 BC, was made with elm, a wood often used by the Romans for their ships. Research has established that the Roman shipwreck discovered at Mahdia, Tunisia, built in elm, measured about 40.6m (133ft) long and 13.8m (45ft) wide. The weight of the ship's marble cargo was estimated at 200 metric tons by the archaeologist Fernand Benoit. The archaeologist Alfred Merlin had estimated the weight at 300 or 400 tons.

The deck, which was about 8in thick, was covered by lead, as was the hull. The construction was of high quality, judging by the wood used and the presence of lead plates. Many bronze nails have also been found during the excavations. Merlin also discovered that the ship was divided into several compartments and possessed vertical dividers. It was assumed that this merchant ship could not sail at the same speed of a warship.

The structure of the ancient Roman oar-ships was generally the same as the other ancient ships, albeit with some differences between types; they had a distinctive *stolos* (prow ornament), although similar to that of the Greek

Detail of the *patera* with representations of *triremes*, 3rd to 2nd century BC. Note the arrangement of the exit holes for the oars (dispersed on three levels), the shields of the soldiers on the naval deck and the apotropaic eyes. The sternposts are straight and stumpy, while the foredeck shows a low bulwark and continues aft until it is masked by the massive shields. The side wall of the foredeck terminated aft with the *parasimon*. The foredeck continues aft over the usual arching side of the cabin to form the maindeck, from the side of which the shields are hanging, over a space two thirds of the depth of the oarbox beneath. According to Morrison the space should represent a ventilation course in its exact position. (Napoli, Museo Archeologico Nazionale, photo D. Carro, courtesy of the museum)

ships. Each ship had a stempost (*prora*); an 'eyebox', an ear-like projection on each side of the bow of the ship formed by a beam lying athwartships at the forward end of the oarboxes, protecting them from damage in bow to bow collision (επωτις); a hull; a planked deck; an upper ram which protected the plating and the keel over the main ram (προεμβολιον); and a gangway (*parodos*, παροδος) on each side of the oared ship, sometimes positioned on the flat upper surface of the oarbox.

Warships could be heavy or light. The broadest warships were the longships (*naves longae*), distinguished from the cargo round ships (*onerariae*). Livy (XXXVII,23,5) distinguishes also between larger (*naves majoris formae*) and smaller ships (*naves minoris formae*). Usually the longships were *rostratae*, i.e. armed with a bronze ram (the *rostrum*), and *cataphractae*, i.e. strongly armoured and protected (*kataphraktos* in Greek, or in Latin *tectus* or *constratus*), meaning that they were fenced in from end to end, with the intention to protect the oarsmen from missiles and/or boarding. The term *machimoi* (μαχιμοι), mentioned by Plutarch in the *Life of Pompeius* (64,1) indicated in general the fighting ships, i.e. armoured *kataphraktoi*. Both terms refer to ships, bigger than *triremes*, built and equipped to take their place in the battle line.

The function of these large Roman warships was to ram enemy ships to provide a firm platform for offensive or defensive action by deck soldiers, and they developed solid and permanent boxing-on – i.e. the wooden structure enclosing the hull of an oared ship with a canopy deck and permanent side-screening to protect the oarsmen from missiles – with louvres for ventilation. 'Cataphracting' a ship meant covering most of the decking and the permanent boxing-on with louvres; this succeeded the earlier Greek-style protection of temporary upper and lower screen panels (in Latin *tectus* and *constratus* meant 'decked'). Many of Agrippa's ships in the campaign against Sextus were made *cataphract*; this was the responsibility of their commander rather than the shipbuilder, probably because the captain of a ship knew better what he needed from his ship during the battle.

Fleets of ships were also known by standard terms depending on type; for example a fleet of fast ships was called *Classis Expedita* (Livy, XXVI,24,1).

Roman *triimiolia*, from the Palazzo Barberini Mosaic. In the mosaic the bow (port and starboard) and the port side of an oared warship are shown with armed marines crowded on the deck behind a bulwark. The sternpost is in Roman style, as in the case of the two-level ship of the Praeneste Relief; in the mosaic no ventilation room is visible but there should be room for it above the oar system and below the deck. (Palestrina, Archaeological Museum, author's photo, courtesy of the museum)

Early Roman warships: undecked *aphractae* and other *pentéconterae*

The first Roman ships were of Etruscan type, as is indicated by the sources: in 394 BC, when the Romans sent an embassy to Delphi, the Roman ambassadors were boarded by Greek pirates of Lipari who, from afar, mistook them for Etruscan pirates. These Etruscan ships were undecked (*aphraktai* or *apertae*, unlike *kataphraktai* and *constratae*). They are clearly visible on the famous crater of Aristhonos, in the Capitolini Museum (see page 10), which depicts an *aphrakta pentecontera* (Greek longship with two levels of oarsmen) fighting against another ship, perhaps a *lembos*, during a naval battle of the second quarter of the 7th century BC. The ships depicted on the Volterra Etruscan Urns often had a single bank of oars, and they do not always show a central deck, only a platform. These undecked ships could, however, be fitted with a fighting ram.

But this does not mean that *pentéconterae* were only of the undecked *aphractae* type. What appears to be a Roman *cataphract pentecontera* with two oar levels is partially visible on the Ficoroni *cista* (Ficoroni bronze casket). This kind of ship, apparently decked but open sided, was fitted with holes for oars (two of the oarports are visible), and was probably a *lembos*. It is interesting to note that, as in this representation of a possible early Roman ship, the deck follows the upcurving stern and is supported by inboard stanchions on each side of the hull, with crosspieces connecting each pair at the tops. However, the deck of this kind of ship was narrower than its beam, and there were no outriggers.

According to Livy (XXXVI,42,8), in 191 BC, the inventory of the fleet of

A

ROMAN *QUINQUEREMES* AND LEMBOS *BIREMES*, 3RD TO 2ND CENTURY BC

1. The reconstruction of a *quinquereme* is based on the coins issued in the 3rd century BC by the Roman republic to celebrate the Romans' new mastery of the sea. Its planked deck ran above the eye panel and the oarbox, of which the coins show the planked side. It had a guard-rail and post from which the rail sloped down to the stempost. In some models the foredeck post was replaced by a tower and it had a double rail. The upper ram ended at the middle wale, below which the lowest wale (doubled in some models) sloped down to the main ram. *Quinqueremes* embarked 30 *nautae* (sailors) and 200 *milites* (legionaries). Note the deep oarbox and oars. On this ship we have reconstructed the 'raven' engine and a copy of one of the *rostra* found in the Aegates Island.

2. The *lembos* (Lat. Lembus, Plautus, Mercator, I,2,81 and II,1,35) was an Illyrian fast ship, probably originally used in piracy and very important for the Romans for its carrying capacity of men, equipment and booty. It could be open and *aphract*, with a strong ramming capacity and rowed at two levels (*biremis*). From this the *liburna* was developed.

1

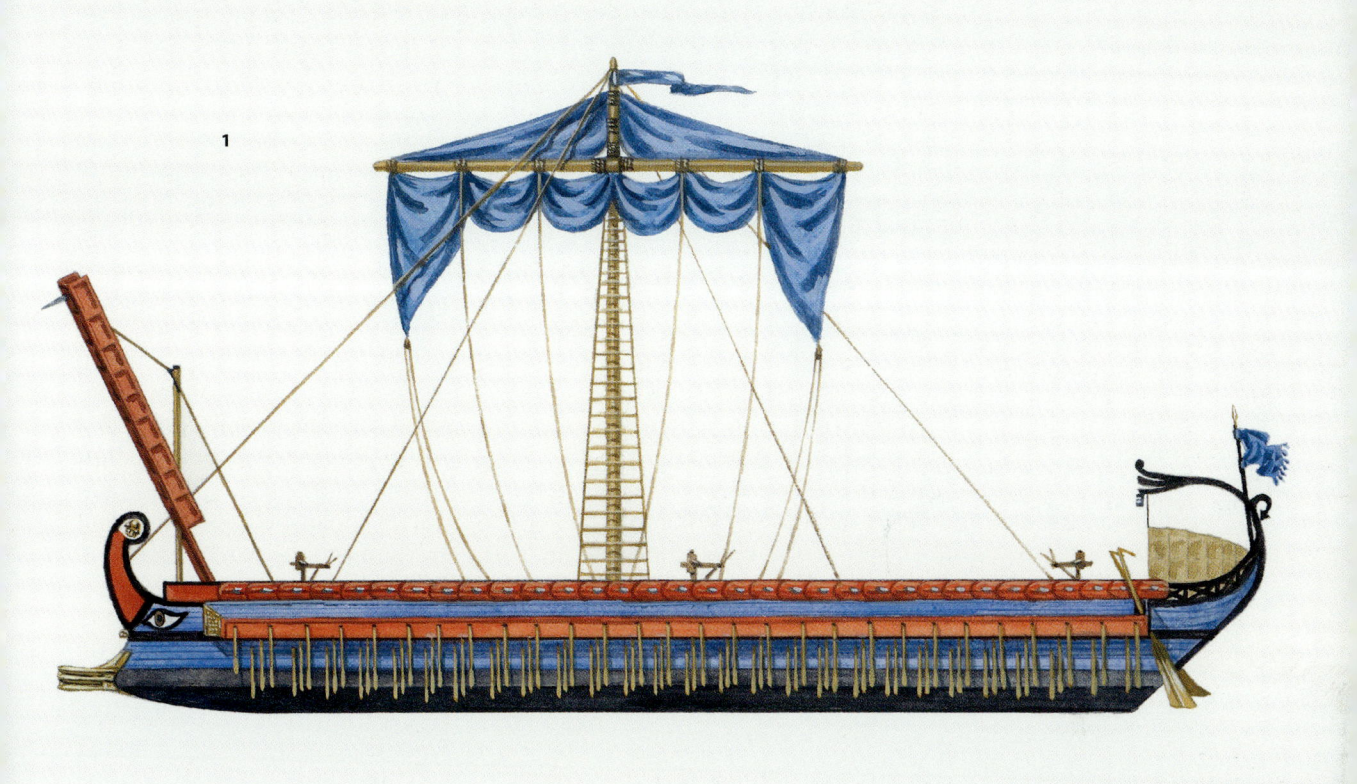

2

Livius, crossing from Peiraieus to Delos to meet Antiochos the Great's fleet at Korykos, included *cataphractae* galleys and many smaller ships (*aphracts*) fitted with rams, and some *naves speculatoriae* without rams. *Aphraktai* were also present in the fleet of Cato the Younger (Plutarch, *Cato the Younger*, 54,3), together with *liburnida* (fast and swift warships) and *kataskopikà* (scout ships): 'Pompey… determined to put the command of his fleet into the hands of Cato, and there were no less than five hundred fighting ships, besides Liburnian craft, look-out ships, and open boats in great numbers.'

The *trireme*

Until the battle of Actium of 31 BC, the *trireme*, belonging to the category of *naves minoris formae*, was one of the main warships of the Roman fleets. This big and heavy warship, based on Greek designs, had three orders of rowers. Virgil (Aeneid,V,119–120) gives us a clear description of the oar working system, saying that a *trireme* is rowed in triple files (*triplici versu*) and the oars rise in three rows. So we have clearly described two aspects of the *trireme*: it had three files of oarsmen a side and three levels of oars. And we learn a rule important for all kind of ship: the number of files of oarsmen gave the ships their names of *trireme*, *quadrireme*, etc.

The Roman sources describe as *hemioliai cataphract* ships which were in reality *triimioliai*. They were often used in place of the *triremes* during the first half of the 2nd century BC. The type was as fast as the *hemioliai* but had an oarcrew of 120 men as compared with the 170 men of the 'Threes'. According to Photius the *triimioliai* were identical to the *triiris* (conventional *trireme*); they had three files of oarcrew a side and can be considered a variety of *trireme*.

The *quadrireme*

The *quadriremes* were the first of the *naves majoris formae*. These larger ships were regularly *cataphractae*, but the *quadriremes* were considered among the lighter types: Cicero, in his *Verrines* (5,89) remembers a *quadrireme* that was incredibly fast under sail. There were two main features: a foredeck unprotected by a bulwark and a main deck with no bulwark, surmounting a latticework ventilation course. They were sometimes rigged with towers, and latticework side-screens in the open side beneath the deck gave some protection. The *quadrireme* could be used sometimes as a scout ship (*navis speculatoria*).

The Alba Fucentia graffito, 1st century BC to 1st century AD. The graffito specifically writes *navis tetreris longa* so clearly evidencing a longship 'Four'. It gives very rough evidence of what a 'Four' looked like from the port side with oars unshipped and mast and sails lowered. (Drawing by Andrea Salimbeti ex Morrison and Coates)

The *quinquereme*

According to many scholars, during the 3rd century BC the first Roman *quinqueremes* of the Punic Wars were larger than their Hellenistic and Punic counterparts, because they were not operated by professional rowers as in the Greek fleets, who were able to manoeuvre three overlapping rows simultaneously;

however, this interpretation, based on an analysis of the coins minted on the occasion of the victories of the First Punic War, is not shared by the scholars Morrison and Coates.

The first Roman *quinqueremes* had the following characteristics: the stempost curved forward and then slightly aft; two oblique bars marked the fitting of the stempost butt to the hull; the eye panel was collocated aft of the stempost. Sometimes the apotropaic eye was unusually high and located at the base of the stempost, as can be seen on later coins of the 2nd century BC. Aft, the *epotis* (επωτις) and a deep oarbox were placed beside each other. In two coin variants, there was no open space above the oarbox between it and the main deck, while in the other two variants, an open side was provided. The open side, screened when necessary against weather and enemy missiles, provided the essential ventilation of this kind of ship. But at the same time, since the heavier models of *quinqueremes* were developed for close combat, defence against missiles was even more necessary. It is possible, then, that some models were conceived with a reduced area of open side, and this characteristic is still visible on the *quinqueremes* of the Ostia relief.

In coins of the Fonteia family, a screened ventilation course is visible towards the stern on the port side, beneath the deck and its guard-rail. Beneath it and above the wale ending in the proembolion the oarbox was built with two levels of oarports, within a machicolated panel. A third course of oarports was inserted above the bottom wale. Sometimes, as visible in the coins of L. Calpurnius Piso, a ventilation course was positioned under the deck with its guard-rail and aft of the stempost fitting and eye panel, running above the assemblage of thick, broad planks, which ends in the proembolion. The three courses of oarports in these models were divided by further wales.

The *quinquereme* was a *longis navis cataphracta* and *rostrata*, belonging to the category of the heavy ships. Weight of ship was strictly correlated with beam, since the length of Roman warships was much the same for different types, and draught would not have varied very much for reasons of stability. The *quinquereme* could sometimes be *expeditae*, i.e. stripped for speed, and then they were regarded as lighter ships.

The bigger *polyremes*

Polyremes of the rating of six and above belonged to the category of the heavy ships. They often acted as flagship, or *navis praetoria*. Silius Italicus, in his poem *Punic* in Book XIV, 487–488, speaking of the siege of Syracuse by Marcellus, fighting against Archimedes and a rescuing Punic fleet, notes that the Roman flagship was a *polyreme* of six orders ('the ship of the Roman commander proceeded faster than the wind pushed by six orders of oars'). Roman flagships, for centuries (from Atilius Regulus to Sextus Pompeius and

Roman *quinqueremes* from the funeral monument of C. Cartilius Poplicola, circa 20 BC. The fragment shows the bow section of a 'Five', with the two rams and back curving stempost, here terminating in a helmeted head, with an oblique line at the juncture with the hull. In the foredeck a marine stands on it behind a planked bulwark. The *parodos* begins outboard of the foredeck bulwark and beneath it follows the apotropaic eye followed by a framed eagle acting as *parasimon*. A wale acts as external support of the *proembolion*. (Ostia, outside Porta Marina, in situ, author's photo)

Reliefs of two Roman *polyremes* with two-level oars, 100 BC. The two ships have two oar levels emerging from beneath what appears to be a heavy rope girdle, but that was in reality a wooden louvre which would be necessary beneath the deck and above the oar system. The ships are portrayed as very large, a 'Nine' or upwards. (Napoli, Museo Archeologico Nazionale, photo D. Carro, courtesy of the museum)

Augustus) were almost always *exeres* (six-banked). So was the *sextera Scipionis*, a *polyreme* with six orders of oars (Livy, XXIX,9,5–8).

Examples of Roman *polyremes*, including a ship of nine orders of oarsmen, are visible on the reliefs of the Napoli Archaeological Museum, showing heavy, single-piece wooden oars manned by multiple oarsmen, but the best sample of a *polyreme*, probably a nine-ordered ship, is that of the Praeneste relief, showing the battle of Actium (see page 18).

Here the lateral face of the hull below the *parodos* shows a course of louvres, which in most *cataphract* ships took the place of the open side. The louvre stands very slightly outboard of the upper course of the oars, both merging as they run forward smoothly, without an *epotis*, with the side wall of the prow. It seems that in the *polyremes* the upper course of the oars in turn was positioned outboard of the lower course of the oars. This short structure of the outriggers – *parexeiresia* – was dictated by the need to build into them a *parodos* for close lateral encounter with enemy ships.

The ancient sources' data on the existence of *polyremes* is backed up by analysis conducted in the last decades on archaeological evidence – in particular, the imposing monument to the victory at Actium built by Augustus in front of Nicopolis, in the area where he had placed his headquarters. On the more than 60m-long (197ft) front wall of the base have been counted 36 or 37 *rostra* of large vessels whose shapes (in cross section) are still largely detectable by the deep grooves etched in stone. While the survey on the fragments visible in the site still continues, the data acquired so far have allowed archaeologists to estimate the total number of *rostra* and, consequently (assuming, according to Murray, a ratio of 1:10), the number of ships captured during the *Bellum Aziacum*. The different sizes of the detectable *rostra* have also provided evidence of the presence of various types of ships bigger than *quinqueremes*, as also reported by the ancient sources. From a virtual reconstruction it has been estimated that the biggest ram detected should have weighed between 2,300kg and 3,800kg, probably for a 'Ten'.

B ROMAN *TRIREMES* AND *QUADRIREMES*, 2ND CENTURY BC

1. The *triremis* was about 120ft long and 15ft wide; it could embark 30 sailors and 120 legionaries. This kind of ship possessed 170 oars, divided in three orders. The *traniti* formed the upper row: they used oars about 12ft in length. The *zigiti* were the oarsmen of the middle row, and managed rows of about 10ft. The *talamiti* formed the lower row with oars 6ft long. The Thranite oarsmen worked their oars through outriggers called *parexeiresia* (παρεξειρεσια). In the Roman 'Three', as shown by the series of Republican coins (*sextants* and *aeres graves*) of *c* and *e* typology of Morrison, these outriggers are inserted in a shallow oarbox. The coins show, above the oarbox, an open space between it and the deck. This open side provided ventilation to the ship.

2. This 'Four' is reconstructed from the Alba Lucentia Graffito, the Urn of Volterra and the coins of the Fonteia family according to the Vierck hypothesis. In good wind conditions, these galleys could reach an excellent speed, thanks to their squared sail, mounted on the single mast. Note the double towers. The 'Fours' represented in the Octavian coins show also a guard-rail along the deck (*parodos*), which is surmounting a panel containing the apotropaic eye, a box with an image (*parasimon*, παρασημον) flanked by the usual X-shaped latticework protecting the open side. The upper oars (*zygian*) would emerge from the hull over the topwale while the oarports would serve the Thalamian oars.

1
2

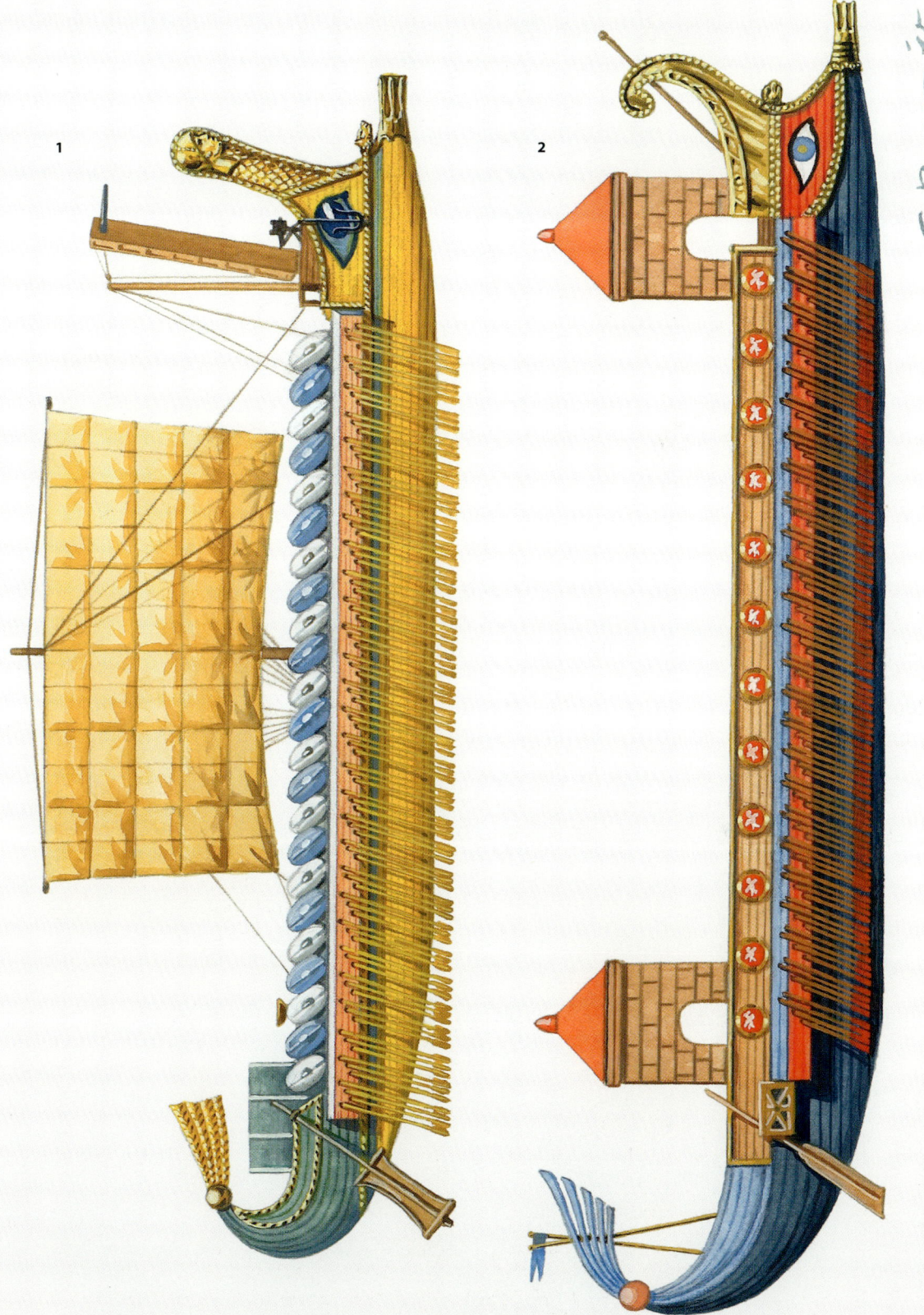

Detail of the Vatican relief, circa 30 BC. The *parasimon* of the ship is a box showing a woman's head (Cleopatra) facing half forward and half sideways. Note the circular symbol on the aft side of the box, representing probably a surrogate of the apotropaic eye of the ship. (Musei Vaticani, Città del Vaticano, author's photo, courtesy of the museum)

Further detail of the previous relief, circa 30 BC. The armed men of the ship stand on the *parodos* (the first two) and behind the bulwark. The gap between the bulwark and the prow wall and *parasimon* was intended to allow the passage onto and out from the deck. (Musei Vaticani, Città del Vaticano, author's photo, courtesy of the museum)

The Lembos *biremes* and the *liburnae*

These famous ships were born on the coast of Dalmatia, a creation of the Illyrian pirates of the Liburni tribe. These Dalmatian Illyrian pirates operated *lemboi* (small ships, usually *biremes*, which were able to catch up with the heavy cargo ships) and *liburnae* (lighter Illyrian pirate ships were named *hemiolia* and *myoparoi*). For naval battles, they used *triremes*. The *liburnae* were originally a type of *cataphract* ship (a two-level *lembos*) which could be used for both fighting and scouting. The type was soon adopted as a warship by the Romans, and the word came to designate types of fast and swift vessels.

Already in 69 BC we find adopted *liburnae* in the Roman fleets, where the fleet of Pompey is described to deploy *liburnides*. Plutarch mentions the *liburnae* in Pompey's fleet as not being fighting ships, so these ships could have been also employed as scout ships (Appian, *Civil Wars* 5,103, *Liburnica* reconnoitring by sea in the fleet of Octavian). Lucan (III,534), describing the ships of Decimus Brutus, admiral of Caesar in 49 BC, said that his fleet included many larger *triremes* and two-level *liburnae*.

The funerary relief of Praeneste, representing a 'Nine' of the battle of Actium, circa 30 BC. The relief is the best representation of a larger two-oar-level oared warship of the Antonius fleet. The crocodile symbol on the wale in the bow, forming a *proembolion*, could indicate that the ship is Egyptian, but crocodile *proembolia* are already visible on the coins of the *Fonteia Gens*. In the bow the stempost curves quickly and then aft in Roman style. Note the tower on the deck and the planked bulwark with the shields. The oar system consisted of 13 massive monoxylous oars in the upper level and 12 (or 13) in the lower level. (Musei Vaticani, Città del Vaticano, author's photo, courtesy of the museum)

The *oneraria*

Cargo ships were used for the transport of troops and military supplies. They navigated solely under sail, towed by the longships, but without an oar system. *Fasili Trieretikì (φασηλοι τριηρετικοι)* was a term for a variety of types. According to Sallust (*Rom. Hist.*, 3,8) a large *phaselus* carried a cohort of 600 men; a *phaselus*, like other intermediary types of auxiliary warships, had oars to enable them to keep up with warships under oar, at ordinary cruising speed. However, they did not have *rostra*. The role of these ships in invasion fleets was fundamental to Roman naval power since the age of the first Punic War.

Other ships

The *myoparones* (μυοπαρονες) were smaller fighting ships, equipped with a ram. This vessel was a longship of the smallest kind with one row of oarsmen on each side. According to Plutarch, Octavianus, at the instigation of his sister Octavia, gave 20 of these ships to his brother-in-law Mark Antony (Plutarch, *Ant.*, 35).

The term *kataskopoi* denotes scout ships, but this may be just a word taken to describe a function, i.e. ships of any type (including *cataphractae*) which performed the function of reconnaissance (*naves speculatoriae*). In fact *quadriremes* or *triremes* or the very fast *liburnians* were the favourite ships for this employment.

The *naves actuariae* were a kind of small oared ship, fitted with rams if necessary for naval warfare (Hirtius, HBA 44). But Livy (XXV,30,10) mentions *actuariae* used as landing craft at the siege of Syracuse. According to Cicero (*Ad Atticum*, 16.3.6) the *actuariae* or *actuariolae* were oared ships of ten oars each, but *actuariae* of more than 30 oars were built.

The *scaphae* were the boats of the large warships. These longboats appear to have been substantial craft that were likely either towed astern or sailed in flotillas. They are usually associated with the *actuariae* and the *speculatoriae* also used to transport light troops and rubble for fortification.

DECORATION AND EQUIPMENT

In the *longae naves* all the oars were fitted with leather sleeves (*askomata*) to avoid water entering when the ship was under sail with the wind abeam, or when the deck soldiers were all fighting on one side of the ship, causing it to heel. It is noteworthy that in such circumstances the oars were pulled in as far as possible.

Liburnian ship of Caesar's army, Aquileia, Metopa of the Great Doric Frieze, 1st century BC. (Aquileia, Museo Archeologico Nazionale, author's photo, courtesy of the museum)

Part of a block for rope and reconstruction, from the wreck of the Roman ship found at Comacchio, last quarter of the 1st century BC. (Courtesy of D.ssa Fede Berti, from the original drawings of the excavations, Ferrara, Archaeological Museum)

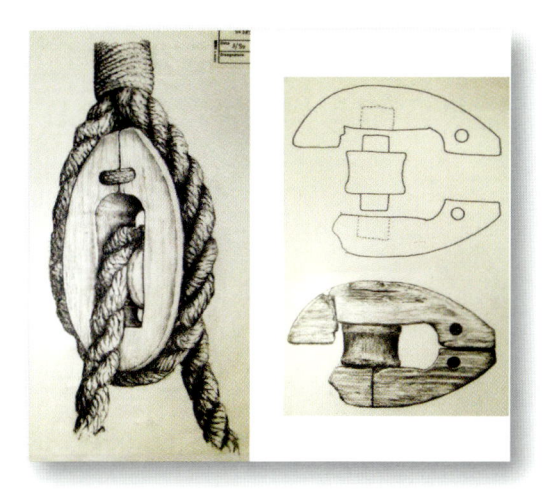

LEFT
Relief showing a prow of *rostrata*, decorated with the Capitoline Wolf-shee, with anchor. (Roma, Musei Capitolini, photo D. Carro, courtesy of the museum)

RIGHT
Proembolion of a Roman trireme, 203 BC, in the shape of a boar's head. This wild boar head was recovered off the port of Genoa in 1597 and brought to Turin after the occupation of Savoy in 1815. It is perhaps linked to the naval operations conducted during the Second Punic War by the Carthaginian general Mago in Liguria, where in 203 BC he was defeated by the Romans, and from where he sailed to return home, but died during the crossing. (Torino, Armeria Reale, photo courtesy of Soprintendenza per le antichità del Piemonte e della Valle d'Aosta)

Colour and decoration

Ovidius (*Met.* XIV, 549–555), while describing the transformation of Aineias's ships into sea nymphs, gives us an important detail on the colour of the certain Roman ships. He says:

> Their rigidity softened, and their wood turned to flesh; the curved sternposts [*puppes*] turned into heads; the oars [*remi*] into fingers and legs, swimming; the sides of each vessel became flanks, and the submerged keel [*carina*] down the ship's middle turned into a spine; the cordage [*lina*] became soft hair, the yards [*antemnae*] were arms; and their dusky [*caerulus*] colour was as before.

Ovidius is clearly describing warships of the 1st century BC or early 1st century AD. The dusky colour of the Roman ships appears to be a constant element through the centuries, because ships of caerulean colour are noted in the age of the Punic Wars and ships of sea blue (*venetus*) colour in the Late Empire are mentioned by Vegetius. The blue (*venetus*) colour was the sacred colour[1] of Neptune, the god of the sea, so probably its use on ships was a holy act in his honour.

Divine elements were strongly present in the decoration of the ships: apotropaic eyes were collocated in their own panel, mainly on the portside and under the *proembolion*, and often the prow of the ship was in the form of a god or a sacred animal, like the ones on the warships carved on the Orange

1 See MAA 451: *Imperial Roman Naval Forces 31 BC–AD 500*, p18–19

C

POMPEY THE GREAT DEFEATS CILICIAN PIRATES, 66 BC

It was Pompey the Great who was to crush the Cilician pirates and give freedom and security to the waterways of the Roman Republic. To do this, Pompey received from the Senate, after long debates, extraordinary powers in 67 BC: the proconsular power (*Imperium Proconsolare*) for three years throughout the Mediterranean basin to the Black Sea with the right to operate up to 45 miles inland. Fifteen legates were put under him with the title of *propraetores* and 20 legions (120,000 men) and 4,000 riders, 270 ships and a budget of 6,000 talents. In a rapid and well-organized campaign he defeated the pirates. Two months sufficed to patrol the Black Sea and root out troublemakers; then it was the turn of Crete and Cilicia (App., *Mithridatic War*, 96). The pirates were destroyed in their own territories and they surrendered to Pompey a great quantity of arms and ships, some under construction, some already at sea, together with bronze, iron, sail cloth, rope and various kinds of timber. In Cilicia 71 ships were taken for capture and 300 for surrender. This scene shows an amphibious operation of Pompey the Great's fleet against the pirates. The main Roman ship is a 'Three'. The burning Cilician ships are two *myoparones* (μυοπαρονες).

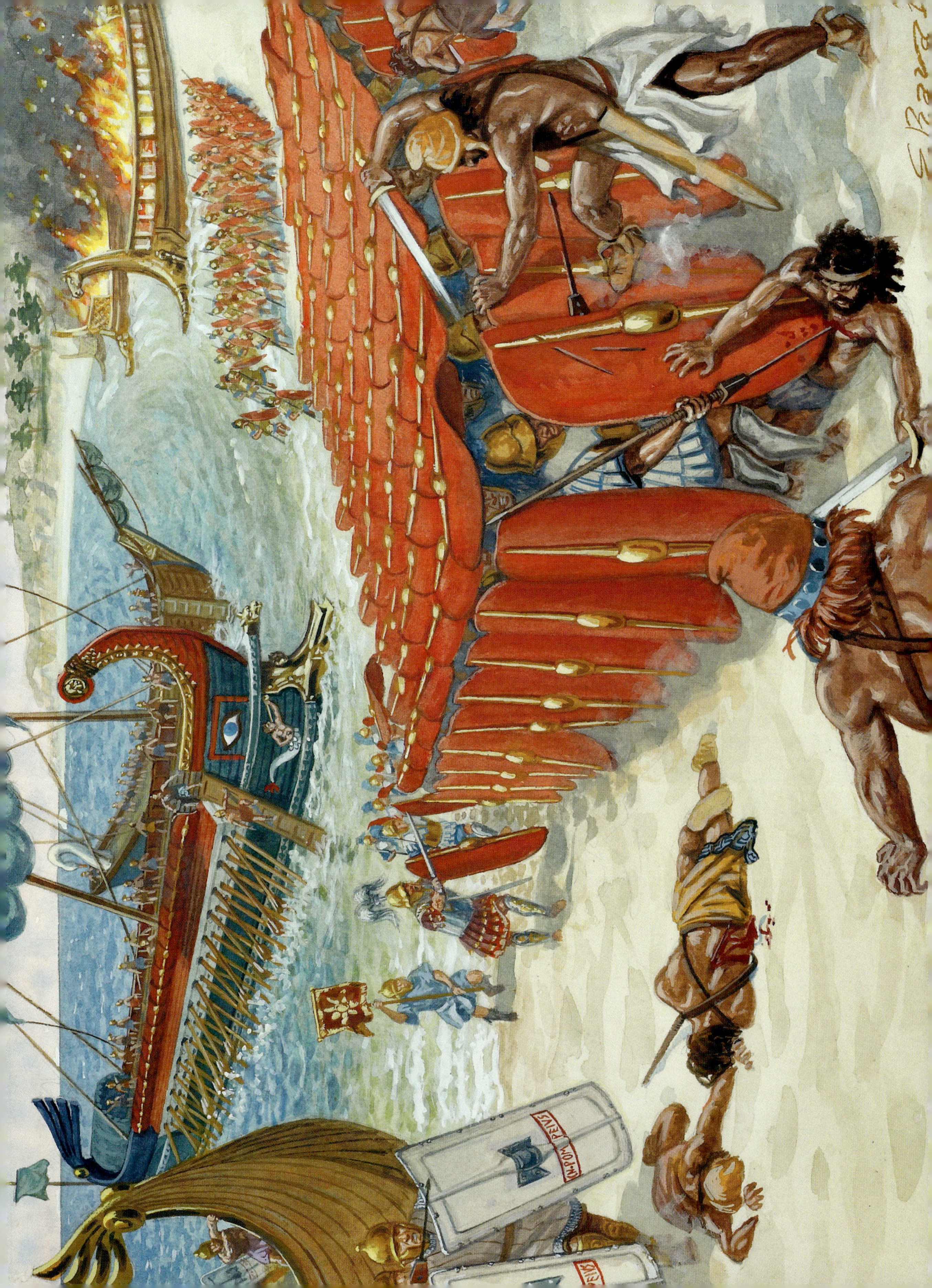

Rostrum of Roman ship, from the site of the Battle of Aegates Islands, bronze, 241 BC, before and after its cleaning. Decorated by a couple of rosettes, this ram was the first *rostrum* found on the battle site during illegal excavations. It was recovered in Trapani by the Italian Carabinieri in 2004, so allowing the Italian archaeologists to find the site of the Aegates battle. The bronze ram is 34in in length and has a slightly different shape to the other rams found in the waters of Levanzo. Indeed, although the rams look similar, all of them are slightly different, the only two almost identical having the same Latin inscription that mentions the same *quaestors*. Analysis of the metal alloy has been carried out on a few rams, and each sample has shown different percentages of the alloy components, i.e. tin, copper, lead and arsenic, plus many minor elements. (Photo courtesy of the Soprintendenza del Mare della Regione Siciliana and RPM Nautical Foundation)

Arch (see page 42). Statues of winged victories stood on the foredeck. Earthen pots and small altars in honour of the gods (*doliola*) identical to the miniature ones found in the Comacchio ship, were sometimes mounted on the stern of warships, as shown in the coins of the Fonteia family. Under the *proembolion* was usually painted or applied the figure of a Triton or a Dolphin. This was the *parasimon* (name-device) of the ship: in that of the Isola Tiberina there were carved, on the *epotis*, the staff and the snake of Asklepios.

Ladders were employed from sailors to go up and down from land to sea. The ladders were prevented from slipping away by a chock placed between their forward side and a possible stanchion inboard, visible for example in the *pentecontor* of Cista Ficoroni at the point where the ladder also is touching the topwale. The dotation of the Comacchio ship has been wonderfully preserved and it has shown us the main instruments and fittings of a ship of late 1st century BC: vessels and amphorae, various pottery and glasses, small altars, garments, shoes and weapons for the crew, leather cases and bags, strigils, cooking tools, lamps, balances, hooks, chains, baskets and fragments of ropes made of canapa, naval wood hammers, cleaning tools. Water containers were carried over the stern. The famous Antikythera mechanism, found on the wreck of an *oneraria* ship of 87 BC, was recently interpreted by Derek de Solla Price as the first naval calendar computer. From the shipwreck of Mahdia we know that the Roman ships had safety equipment, pump and four or five large anchors.

ARMAMENT AND TACTICS

The ram

An armed ship was called *navis ornata* (Livy,43.9.4). The main offensive weapon of the ship was the bronze element of its *prora* (*prorae aeratae*, Verg., Aen.,X, 223), the ram or *rostrum*. All *cataphract* ships would have been equipped with a *rostrum*. Recent archaeological discoveries have finally brought to light true specimens of Roman and Carthaginian *rostra*, from the Aegates battle site, while a *rostrum* linked to the clashes between Agrippa and Sextus Pompeius's fleets has been recently found near Messina and Acqualadroni. The famous *rostrum* of Athlit (weighing 600kg) is not Roman but Hellenistic, although it is identical to those used by Mark Antony at the battle of Actium and dedicated in the Nicopolis monument.

This big armoured ram on the prow transformed the oar-ship into a formidable war machine. It was positioned on the waterline or underwater, and was an integral part of the prow to which it was attached by mortise. Most often the enemy's ship would be sunk by the impact of the *rostrum*, but if it was manoeuvrable and commanded by an able officer it could take the blow at an oblique angle and survive. In anticipation of ram tactics Agrippa armoured his ships with metal plates before his war against Sextus Pompeius.

The 'raven'

During the first two Punic Wars (264–242 and 218–202 BC) the Carthaginians trusted mainly to ramming and a quick disengagement as their main offensive tactic. To counter it, the Romans developed some sophisticated systems to ensure that the ramming ship could not disengage after the attack, and therefore give the embarked Roman infantry the chance to board and fight hand-to-hand on its deck. But as ropes attached to grappling hooks could easily be cut with a knife, the *Consul* Caius Duilius (according to tradition) created a machine which combined the function of grappling hook and boarding pontoon. Near the prow of the galley a small mast was built, against which a hinged gangway was mounted vertically. Under the end of the gangway was fixed a heavy iron harpoon, called *corvus* ('the raven') or *korax*, which could penetrate the deck of the enemy's ship when the gangway was brought down on it; the Roman infantry could then cross it and board the enemy's ship.

It has been said that to board an enemy ship with a 'raven' was a more complex manoeuvre than to ram her or mow down her oars. But first of all

Detail of the previous ram, showing the decorative rosettes. Concentrated in a precise area, the rams have allowed the archaeologists to identify the point where the two opposing fleets clashed in the decisive battle of the First Punic War. Formed from a single piece cast in bronze, the *rostrum* was firmly attached to the wooden bow of the ship by numerous nails of which traces remain on the board, at the junction between the forward end of the keel and the lowest side of the stem. The front part is constituted by a powerful vertical slash strengthened by three horizontal laminas shaped like blades of a trident. (Photo courtesy of the Soprintendenza del Mare della Regione Siciliana and RPM Nautical Foundation)

Another *rostrum* of Roman ship, found near Levanzo, possible site of the battle of Aegates Islands, bronze, 241 BC. This *rostrum*, cast in bronze, is about 27in long and was recovered in the same site as the previous one by the Soprintendenza del Mare della Regione Siciliana, Dr. Sebastiano Tusa, and the RPM Nautical Foundation, assisted by nautical means of the Department of Naval Air of Guardia di Finanza, at the end of June 2008. Up until 4 July 2014, 11 rams have been recovered from the site.(Photo courtesy of the Soprintendenza del Mare della Regione Siciliana and RPM Nautical Foundation)

we should note that Romans trained for such manoeuvres. And the structure itself of ships like the *quinqueremes* was favourable to the use of such engines, as well as to embark fighting troops. If the Roman *quinqueremes* – larger than the Carthaginian ones – were on one hand more 'difficult to operate' as Polybius noted, then their advantage was that they were more stable and allowed the presence of a large naval infantry force, and of course, the use of the 'raven'. Besides the classic 20 marines, recruited from the maritime allies (*naval socii*), the Romans embarked on each ship 80 legionaries – a complete *centuria*, but trained to fight on the sea.

Turrets

Turrets could be mounted on ships with offensive and defensive purpose. Warships' turrets were all painted differently, probably as a way of distinguishing them; at the battle of Naulocos in 36 BC Agrippa could tell that more than half of Sextus Pompeius's fleet had been destroyed by counting the different colours of the towers still visible on the enemy ships. Agrippa introduced some innovative features, such as detachable combat towers that could be quickly erected on the deck. Catapults, *ballistae*, and *scorpiones* (a type of war machine also called a triggerfish) were the usual war machines mounted on the main deck, over and inside the turrets. Protective side-screening materials like leather or horsehair would be kept rolled up, and when needed let down to cover both the open sides and the oars at the point of emergence from the oarbox. In some coins of the Fonteia family this protective material is even visible on two levels.

Agrippa's technicians invented a new weapon to hook up a ship from a distance. This new weapon was called a *harpax*, and was a large beam, more than 2m long, iron-covered for protection against axe blows. At each end it was fitted with a strong ring. To one ring was fastened an iron hook, while the other ring was linked to a thick rope. It helped to accelerate collisions and subsequent boardings. The *harpax* was sent through a catapult, and when its hook gripped, the rope was retracted with a pulley, so that the two ships were pulled together and the soldiers could board. It worked very well until a counter was invented: a large blade, attached to a long pole, which cut the rope.

D **ROMAN *HEMIOLIA* AND *QUINQUEREMES*, 69 BC**
Two ships from Pompey the Great's fleet.

1. The *hemiolia-triimiolia* is based on the ship of the Palazzo Barberini Mosaic of Palestrina. It has been reconstructed with oars dispersed on two levels, an *echelon* to judge from the forward pair of which the lower oars are visible forward of the upper oars, on the original mosaic. This feature links with the ship of the Palazzo Spada Relief, representing a Hellenistic *triimiolia*, probably Egyptian, and with the Rhodian ship of the Samothracia victory. The ship has 52 oars a side, a quarter double-manned, and an oarcrew calculated by Morrison as 130 rowers (26 + 26 + 13 per side). This kind of ship was about 60ft long.

2. A reconstruction of a 'Five' based on the Isola Tiberina monument, ex Coates, supplied with the colours of Pompei 'Fives': it has 282 oarsmen, but, as suggested by Morrison, their number could be elevated to 300, by adding two more rooms to the length (about 130ft) and having two men to each oar. Note the oarbox with horizontal top and the *parodos*; the presence of the latter limits the use to which the space under the main deck can be put to accommodate oarsmen, but it has its value in attack or defence in boarding battles between heavily armed ships. The *thranite* oars are fitted with *paraxeiresia*. The *rostrum* here reconstructed, in both ships, is the one found in Acqualadroni, near Messina. In the *quinqueremes* it was apparently above the waterline (*avasteiros, αναστειρος*).

1

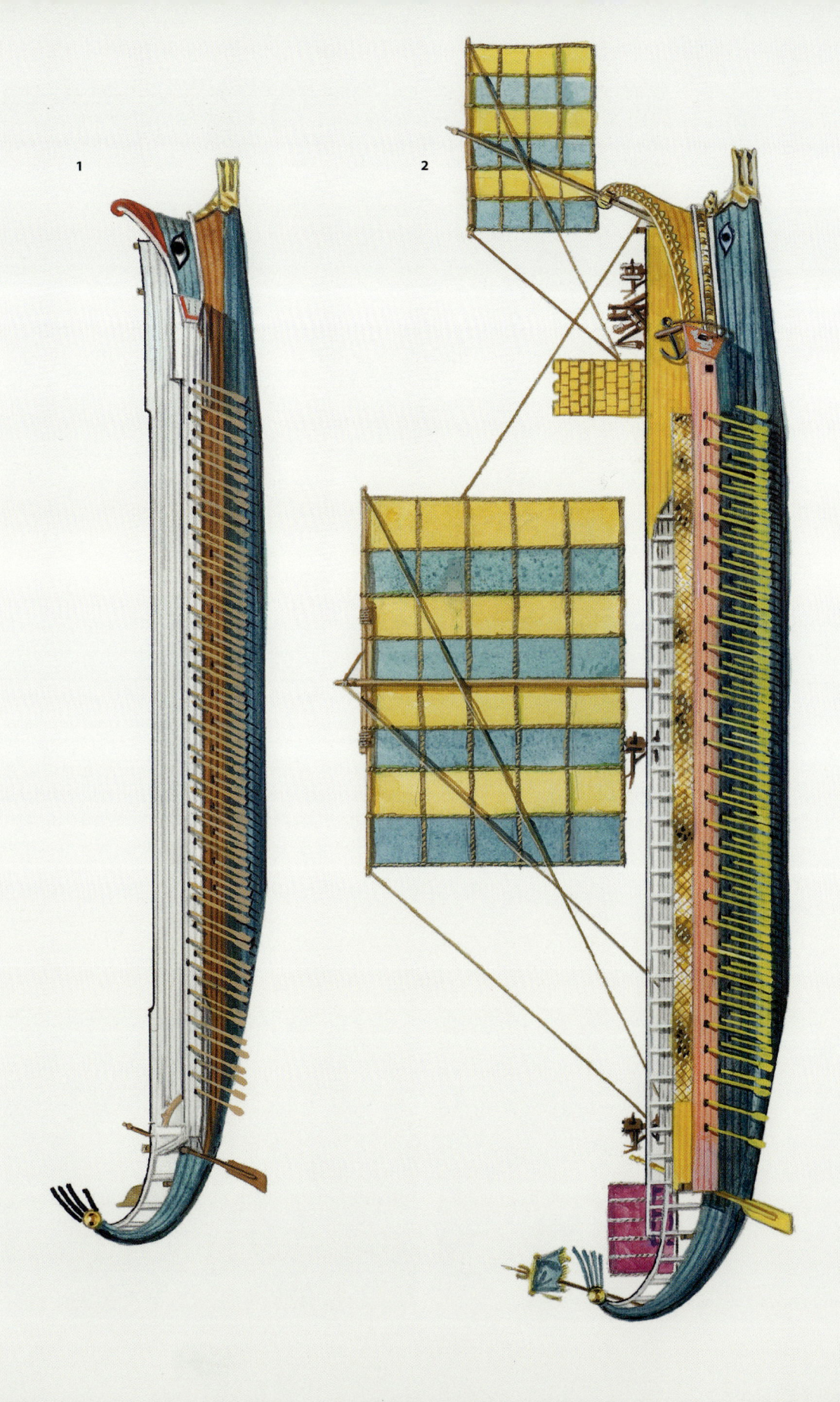

2

Front view of the previous ram. The function of the ram was to create holes in enemy ships: located at the junction between the forward end of the keel and the lowest part of the straight bow and nailed to the wood hull, in the impact with the enemy ship the ram created deadly damage due to vertical and horizontal swipes. (Photo courtesy of the Soprintendenza del Mare della Regione Siciliana and RPM Nautical Foundation)

Roman *rostrum*, decorated with a winged victory and reporting the inscription *C(aio) PAPERIO Ti(berii) F(ilio) M(arco) POPULICIO L(ucii) F(ilio), Q.P.* (Photo courtesy of the Soprintendenza del Mare della Regione Siciliana and RPM Nautical Foundation)

Fighting on the sea: Roman naval tactics

The Romans' reliance on hand-to-hand fighting to win naval victories resulted in the return of old-fashioned tactics, based on infantry fighting. Firstly manoeuvring in a skilled way to gain a favourable position, the two contenders skirmished with spears, javelins, arrows and slings. The canopy deck of the ship accommodated the longship's secondary armament of archers and armed men, equipped with hand weapons and missiles, and later with catapults.

When the position was gained, the main aim was to ram the enemy's ship, and once the Roman soldiers had boarded the enemy's vessel, the hand-to-hand fighting began with daggers, swords, spears, axes and maces. The protection of the fighters was mainly trusted to their shield and their armour, if worn.

Generally oars alone were used during fighting, although under exceptional circumstances – like in the battle between the Roman Livius and Polyxenidas, admiral of Antioch the Great – the smaller foresail was raised in or before battle.

Roman *rostra*, decorated with a Montefortino helmet and inscribed QVINCTIO QVAISTOR PROBAVET. The first ram of this typology was the first *rostrum* which was recovered from the sea in the summer of 2012. On the top of the band which covers the stem is embossed a helmet of the Montefortino type, conical, with cheek-pieces, apex, and three feathers. The helmet, made in relief at the time of the fusion, reproduces the type in use evidenced by archaeological findings related to the battle. It surmounts the inscription, also made at the time of the fusion, but impressed in negative. The text, in analogy with the previous one, would indicate the name and the position of the two magistrates (*quaestores*) responsible for supervising the implementation of the melting. (Photo courtesy of the Soprintendenza del Mare della Regione Siciliana and RPM Nautical Foundation)

Prow of warship, graffito on the frescoed walls of the Anfushi Necropolis. The realistic details of this graffito may have been be traced by some Caesarian soldier, and show the prow of a huge warship with fighting tower fitted with a fired brazen. (in situ Alexandria, Egypt, photo courtesy Admiral Carro)

The Romans knew well the Greek manoeuvres of the *Periplous* and *Diekplous*: the first tactic, usually employed by a fleet which had a more consistent number of ships than its enemy, consisted in pinning the opponent with a front attack and extending one flank sideways, then rounding in a position from which the enemy flank and rear could be menaced. In the second tactic (fitted for faster ships), a warship in the centre of the attacker's line would race for a gap between two enemy ships, closely followed by a second one: at the opportune moment the first ship would have put its helm over and would scrape the side of one enemy, destroying its oars and causing it to slew. At that point the second warship could ram the disabled enemy. The attacking fleet would then have poured into the resulting gap and would have fallen upon the rest of the opponent's navy.

ROWING A ROMAN WARSHIP

Rower disposition

The key to reconstructing the Roman oar system is to understand the disposition of the oarsmen. According to Vitruvius (I,2,4) the Latin word *interscalmium* should be considered together with the Greek words *Triērēs* (*Triremis*) and *Triskalmos* (i.e. 'with three tholepins', synonymous of *Triērēs*). *Interscalmium* is the term for the longitudinal distance between one rowlock and the next two in a fore-and-aft file of oarsmen (i.e. the oarsmen's room), called in Greek *dipheciaca*. One theory of how oarsmen on a *trireme* would be arranged suggests that their seating planks were arranged as ladders, with each row positioned lower from inboard to outboard. Another theory places the rowers *traniti* and *zigiti* seated side by side on an upper plank, with the oars passing through different holes of the wood wall, while the rowers *talamiti* sat on a lower plank.

On the later Roman *quinquereme*, with about 160 oars divided into three orders, 270–300 rowers were divided into 60 teams of five men each (hence *quinque-remis*), divided into three rowers with one oar and two to another. We should suppose that inside each team there was some sort of chief. He was probably the most experienced rower, or possibly the sturdiest; he would have sat at the front end of the oar operated by his teammates, who emulated his movements. By analogy, among all the 60 teams of paddlers, the first two, those who sat in the stern most directly in contact with the *hortator*, had to be the best and the most trusted. The oar stroke, which due to the length and weight of the oars had to be very short, happened, like today, in four phases: entry into the water; passage in the water; extraction; and recovery.

Detail of a sailor's equipment on an Etruscan Urn, 3rd century BC. (Volterra, Museum Guarnacci, author's photo, courtesy of the museum)

Keeping rhythm

The rhythm was marked by a man called the *pausarius*, with the hammer (*portisculus*) or with verses in hexameters (the so-called *celeuma*). From the *celeuma* reported in the *Latin Anthology* (ed. Mackail, p. 62, attributed to Saint Colomban 543–615 AD, but probably derived from a very ancient one) we can found certain characteristics as working hypotheses. The song is divided into four *tetrastichi* or quadruplets of hexameters, each of which begins with the same expression: *Heia viri, nostrum reboans echo sonet heia!* Following

E — THE SIEGE OF SYRACUSE, 212 BC

The scene shows two Roman warships flanked attacking the walls of Syracuse with over-mounted engines and towers. The Roman fleet at the siege relied mainly on 'Fives', although Silius Italicus (*Punica*, XIV) mentions Roman *triremes*, one of them – manned by Cuman allies under the command of Corbulo – decorated with the statue of the goddess Venus on the foredeck. In the description of the siege Livy (XXIV,34,4–12) and Silius agree that the Roman commander Marcellus used pairs of 'Fives' lashed side by side, carrying siege towers and engines (*sambucae*). In the assault, slingers, archers and javelin throwers fought from his ships.

These *sambuca* siege ladders had a stage on the top, with soldiers moved by pulleys; these devices allowed the Romans to attack the high walls of the Greek city. However, the assault was opposed by the 'iron hands' of Archimedes. During the siege Marcellus used four *sambucae* on four pairs of *quinqueremes*. The ladder mounted on the platform and lashed-together vessels was the shape of a *sambuca*, a musical instrument similar to the *kithera*. According to Polybius (*Rom. Hist.*, VIII,4,4–10): 'A ladder was made four feet broad, and of a height to reach the top of the wall from the place where its foot had to rest; each side of the ladder was protected by a railing, and a covering or pent-house was added overhead. It was then placed so that its foot rested across the sides of the lashed-together vessels, which touched each other with its other extremity protruding a considerable way beyond the prows. On the tops of the masts pulleys were fixed with ropes: and when the engines were about to be used, men standing on the sterns of the vessels drew the ropes tied to the head of the ladder, while others standing on the prows assisted the raising of the machine and kept it steady with long poles. Having then brought the ships close in shore by using the outer oars of both vessels they tried to let the machine down upon the wall. At the head of the ladder was fixed a wooden stage secured on three sides by wicker-shields, upon which stood four men who fought and struggled with those who tried to prevent the *sambuca* from being made to rest on the battlements.'

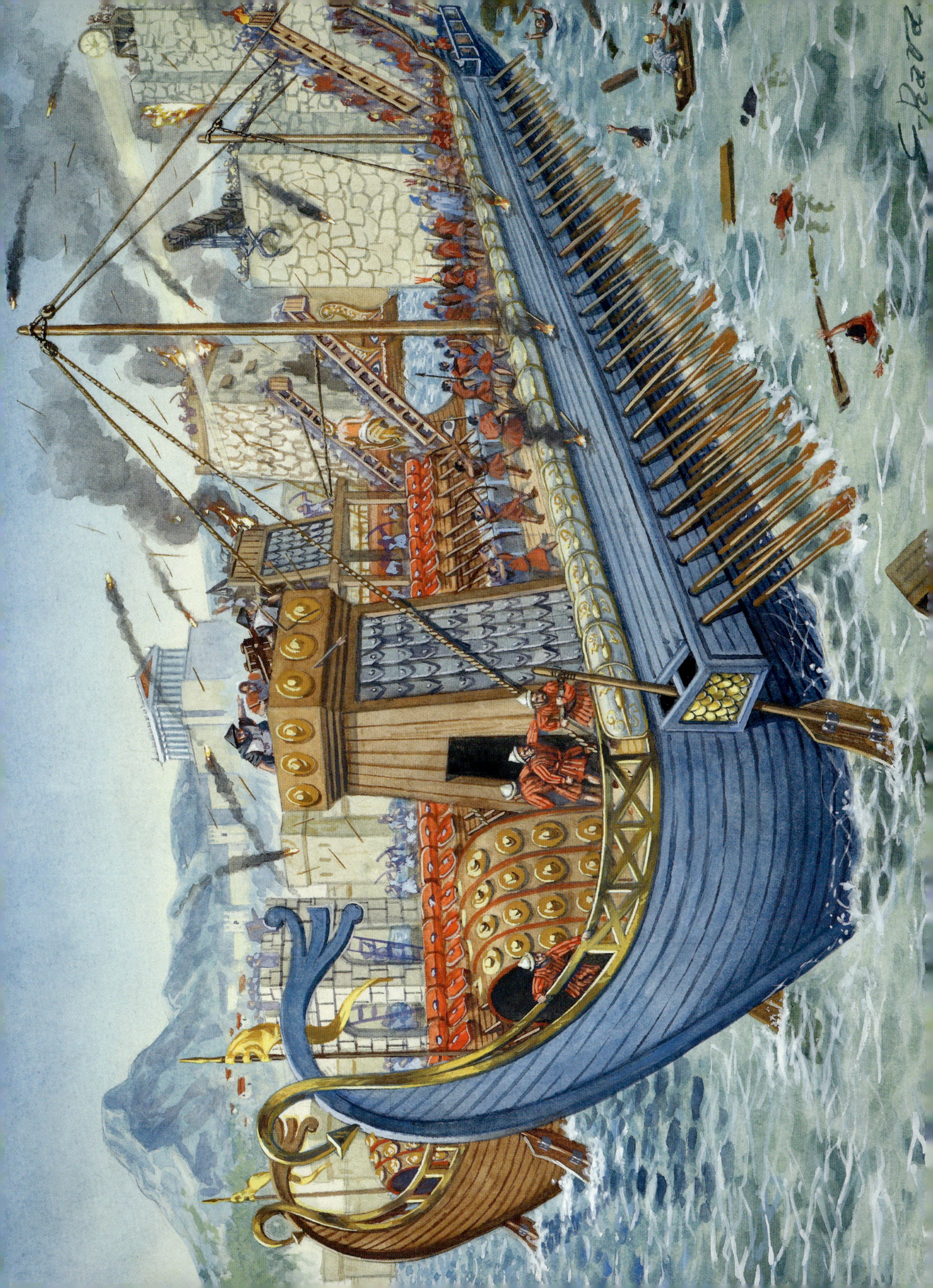

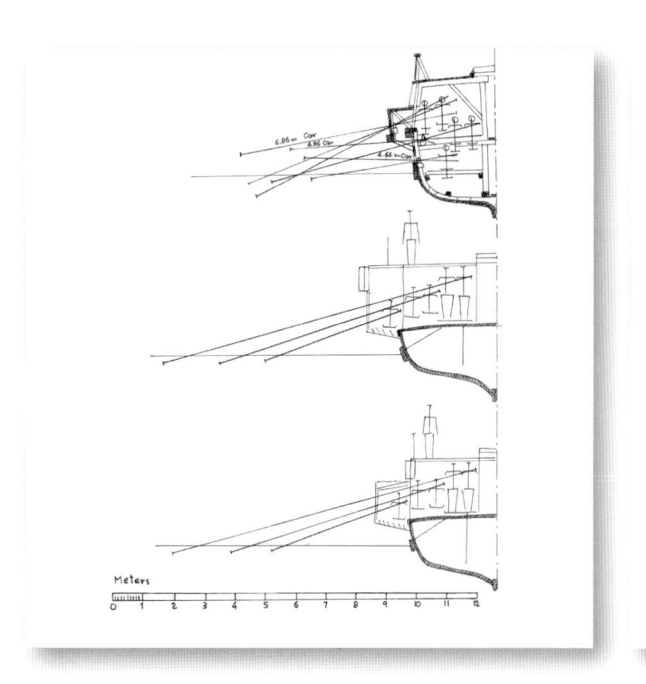

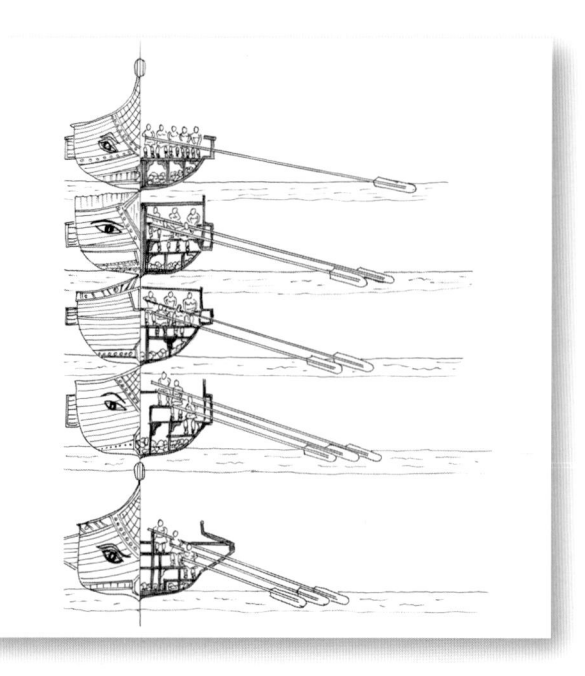

LEFT
Rowing schema, from top to bottom: a) Ship of the Isola Tiberina monument as a 'Five'; b) Ship of Poplicola monument as a 'Five'; c) Ship of Republican coin as a 'Five'. (Drawing by Andrea Salimbeti ex Morrison and Coates)

RIGHT
Rowing schema, from top to bottom: a) Roman *quinquereme* of the First Punic War; b) *Quinquereme* of second type; c) *Quinquereme* from Praeneste; d) *Trireme* of first type; e) *Trireme* of second type. (Drawing by Andrea Salimbeti ex Henniquiau and Martin)

the rhythm of the *hortator*, the oarsmen probably sang the other three lines of the quatrain, and then the word came back again to the *hortator* who repeated the first hexameter of the next quatrain. Singing in rhythmic manner while marching or exercising is very natural for a man. It is distracting, relieves fatigue and helps to avoid mistakes in the movements. Probably the *celeuma* (this or another equivalent) was sung during what we can call 'cruise speed', while during combat absolute silence was demanded, and they proceeded at the sound of the hammer. Now, if one recites the first verse above indicated with the metric and with the breaks of the hexameter, it should sound like this:

Heia viri / nostrum reboans / echo sonet heia!

The pauses divide it into three distinct parts, each consisting of two feet. Every part, proclaimed very slowly with its syllables in arsis and thesis and its ruptures or metric breaks, may correspond to a stroke of the oars, according to this scheme:

- *Heia viri*: entry into the water and passing in the water;
pause: extraction and recovery;
- *Nostrum reboans*: entry into the water and passing in the water;
pause: extraction and recovery;
- *Echo sonet heia*: entry into the water and passing into the water.

On this basis some scholars have suggested that the *celeuma*'s rhythms normally counted 15–16 strokes per minute, one every 4 seconds, which can be increased to 20 if you pronounce the *celeuma* faster. As the song is composed of 16 hexameters, and each hexameter includes three row strokes, the total recitation of the *celeuma* implies 48 entering into the water and then a little more than three minutes of rowing, after which the rowers started again from the beginning.

CAMPAIGNS

The First Punic War

The first major naval conflict fought by the Romans was the First Punic War (264–242 BC), and it was in this war that an effective Roman navy (*classis*) first appeared. For at least 70 years the Romans had their own navy, although very small, and they could also rely upon the ships of the major naval maritime cities of Italy (mainly the ports of Campania and Taranto). Now, however, they had to challenge the most powerful existing maritime power in the western Mediterranean, Carthage.

At the start of the First Punic War, the typical ships in the Mediterranean were *quadriremes* and *quinqueremes*, of which all the navies of the eastern Mediterranean kingdoms, and those of Carthage and Syracuse in the west, were widely equipped. But Rome had only small ships without a bridge (*aphraktoi*); they lacked even the *lemboi* (pirate ships with 50 oars) or long vessels (patrol or surveillance ships, *naves speculatoriae*). This is at least what Polybius noted, with dismay, although we have seen that some *triremes* were present in the Roman fleet. The Romans had absolutely no experience of the construction of *quinqueremes*, because until then in Italy this kind of ship was rarely employed.

At this time, only the Strait of Messina separated the Punic territories from the Roman ones; the last treaty between Rome and Carthage had banished the Punics from Italy and the Romans from Sicily. However, conflict broke out in 265 BC in Sicily between Italian mercenaries of the former tyrant (the *Mamertines*, or 'Servants of Mars') and the forces of Hiero II, the new ruler of Syracuse. Facing defeat, the mercenaries appealed to first Carthage and then Rome for support, but by the time Rome decided to intervene Carthaginian warships and troops had sailed into Messina, the mercenaries' besieged stronghold.

In 264 BC, a strong Roman army arrived under the command of the *Consul* Appius Claudius. The Roman commander, blocked from landing due to the Carthaginian presence in the Straits of Messina, spread the word that he could not continue the war, and pretended to withdraw all his fleet to Italy (Frontinus, 1). The Romans then asked their allies Tarentini, Locresi, Eleatics and Neapolitans to lend them 50-oared ships, *triremes* as well as other types of oared warships, and on those, with serious risk, they ferried their men to Sicily. The Carthaginians attacked them in the Straits, and a *cataphract* ship ran aground and fell into the hands of the Romans.

THE *CELEUMA*

It is interesting to quote the whole text of the *celeuma*.

HEIA, VIRI, NOSTRUM REBOANS ECHO SONET **HEIA**!
ARBITER EFFUSI LATE MARIS ORE SERENO
PLACATUM STRAVIT PELAGUS POSUITQUE PROCELLAM,
EDOMITQUE VAGO SEDERUNT PONDERE FLUCTUS.
HEIA, VIRI, NOSTRUM REBOANS ECHO SONET **HEIA**!
ANNISU PARILI TREMAT ICTIBUS ACTA CARINA
NUNC DABIT ARRIDENS PELAGO CONCORDIA CAELI
VENTORUM MOTU PRAEGNANTI CURRERE VELO.
HEIA, VIRI, NOSTRUM REBOANS ECHO SONET **HEIA**!
AEQUORA PRORA SECET DELPHINIS AEMULA SALTU
ATQUE GEMAT LARGUM, PROMAT SESEQUE LACERTIS,
PONE TRAHENS CANUM DEDUCAT ET ORBITA SULCUM.
HEIA, VIRI, NOSTRUM REBOANS ECHO SONET **HEIA**
AEQUOREOS VOLVENS FLUCTUS RATIS AUDIAT **HEIA**!
CONVULSUM REMIS SPUMET MARE. NOS TAMEN **HEIA**!
VOCIBUS ADSIDUIS LITUS REDUCI SONET **HEIA**!

So, from a more technical point of view, we could translate:

Heia men, echo resounding send back our heia!
Placid lies the wide-spread floor of the sea: the tempest,
calmed by the serene face of the Ocean's arbiter, slumbers;
Under their sliding weight, conquered, the waves are quiet.
Heia men, echo resounding send back our heia!
Beat with your equal oar-stroke, steadily shake the keelson!
Soon the smiling agreement of the sky with the sea shall allow us to run
under our bellying sail, with the wind's swift motion.
Heia men, echo resounding send back our heia!
So that our emulous prow may cut the waves like a dolphin,
row till the timbers groan and the ship leap under your muscles
backward our whitened path flows in a lengthening furrow.
Heia men, echo resounding send back our heia!
Sweeping the waves play the Phorci: sing we, however heia!
Stirred by our strokes the sea foams; we still heia!
Voices unwearying, echo along the shore, sing heia!

Roman *assis*, 3rd century BC, representing the prow of a *quinquereme* or 'Five', Medagliere of Museo di Antichità di Torino, concession of *Ministero dei beni e delle attività culturali e del turismo*. The 'Prow series' of the Roman coins attests the public proclamation of the republic's awareness of her position as a naval power and is accordingly dated to the period of the First Punic War, or slightly later. This is the variant *d* in the classification of Morrison. Note the club of Hercules displayed on the vertical side of the foredeck. Although here it is scarcely visible, there is a tower with guard-rails. The deck reaches the edge of the die and may be regarded as continuous, with a main deck after its planked side giving place to an open side. (© Soprintendenza per i Beni Archeologici del Piemonte e del Museo Antichità Egizie)

This was the ship that would form the basis of the new Roman fleet.

Over the next year, Rome gained control of many Sicilian territories, gaining allies and successfully besieging and looting the Carthaginian army's camp. But Carthage was still ruler of the sea, and the Roman ships could not match the powerful five-banked Punic vessels. Seeing that the war now hung in the balance, and that Africa was left completely unscathed, the Romans finally realized that the outcome of the war would be decided on the sea and decided to deal with the Carthaginians there. The sources tell us that the Romans had a *coup de chance*: the Punic *Triera* (according to Polybius *quinqueremes* or *pentères*) captured by Appius. The Roman shipbuilders dismantled it piece by piece and copied it piece by piece. In the course of a few weeks, 160 vessels were built of green wood – 100 *quinqueremes* and 20 *triremes*, with the others probably of minor size.

In record time the Roman *Res Publica* had built its own powerful navy, which was mainly manned by naval allies (*socii navales*). The command of the fleet was given to Gnaeus Cornelius Scipio. At the battle of Lipara, however, in 260 BC, a squadron of 17 Roman ships under the command of Cornelius Scipio was captured by 20 Carthaginian ships.

After this defeat, the other Roman *Consul*, Caius Duilius, was given command, and he invented the *corvus* assault bridge. At this time, according to Polybius, Roman ships were still poorly constructed and difficult to manoeuvre; Duilius's new assault bridge allowed the inexperienced Romans to counter the Carthaginians' expertise in seamanship and ramming tactics with a seaborne infantry attack, of the kind at which they were masters.

The new weapon was soon used at the battle of Mylae (nowadays Milazzo), on the western coast of Sicily, in one of the turning points of the First Punic War. The Punic admiral, Hannibal, was reconnoitring with his fleet when he fell in unexpectedly with a superior force of the Romans. Hannibal, despising his enemy, bore down upon it without arraying his ships in the usual battle order. As soon as they came near the Roman warships the Carthaginians' first ships were grappled by the new machines, and the boarding Roman infantrymen poured in from the war vessels. The Carthaginians were taken by surprise and overpowered, and lost 30 ships of the vanguard. When the other ships tried to approach, the grappling-irons hung over them, and another 50 Punic warships were sunk. Hannibal managed to escape in an open boat. The command of the western sea, which Carthage had enjoyed for centuries, had now passed to a foe who had first taken to it only a few months before.

F — THE BATTLE OF THE AEGATES ISLANDS, 10 MARCH 241 BC

The scene shows Roman and Carthaginian *quinqueremes* clashing in the midst of the battle which marked the end of the First Punic War. The Roman legionaries are using the famous 'raven'; this pontoon, 18ft long and 4ft broad, was attached to a pillar of wood set up by the bowsprit, from which it was dropped when the two ships came in contact. Its end was fitted with a sharpened bar of iron, which was driven by the force of the fall into the enemy's deck. When the ships were laid broadside to broadside, the Roman soldiers, embarked on the ships, jumped from all parts of their own ship onto the Punic one; when prow touched prow, they went two and two along the gangway, protected by their shields. Note the larger size of the Roman 'Five'. It is highly possible that the Roman *quinqueremes* had oarboxes larger and deeper than the Carthaginian and Hellenistic ships, able to accommodate a three-level oar system.

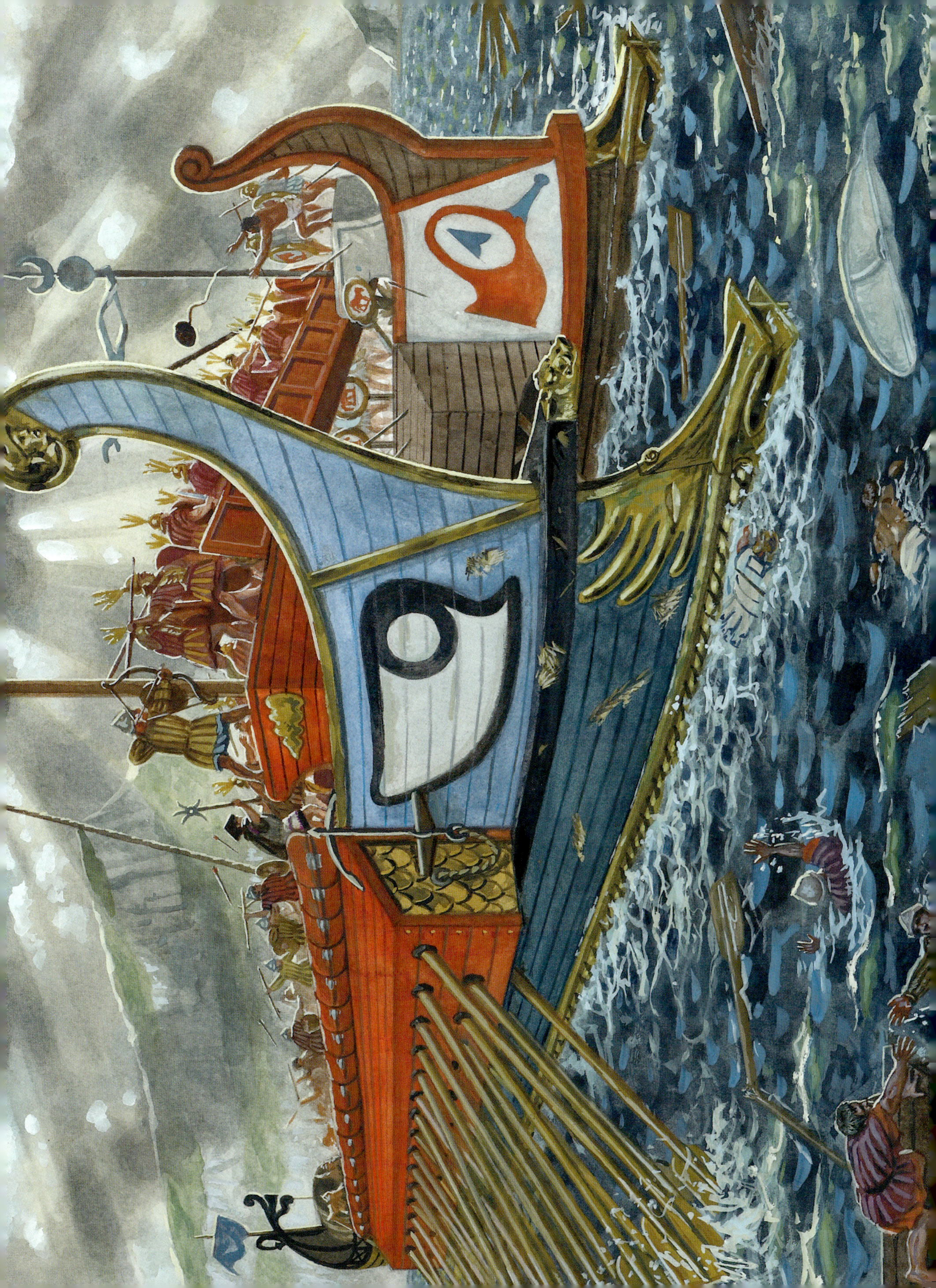

Relief showing a prow of *rostrata*, with the *proembolion* decorated with the head of a wolf. Note, in the frieze, the detailed representation of the helm, the swan shaped *aplustre* (stern) and the anchor. (Roma, Musei Capitolini, photo D. Carro, courtesy of the museum)

Helmet of Montefortino type, found near the site of the Aegates Islands, 241 BC, after cleaning. Various helmets of the so-called Montefortino category were found on the site of the Aegates battle: bronze, domed, with short rear neck protector and an apical button, on which were stuck feathers or a plume of horsehair making them look taller and terrifying. Such helmets, of Celtic origin, were used by the Roman marines up to the 1st century AD. These specimens were part of the defensive equipment of the Roman army during the battle, but similar helmets were used also by the Carthaginian army. (Photo courtesy of the Soprintendenza del Mare della Regione Siciliana and RPM Nautical Foundation)

After some months Hannibal sailed to Sardinia, where he was again confronted by the Roman fleet; miserably beaten, he tried to escape but was captured by the survivors of his own fleet and crucified. In 256 BC the Senate of Rome, tired of the long campaign, decided to carry the war into Africa. A fleet of 330 decked ships was built, on which the Romans embarked their best troops. Each warship had a crew of 300 sailors and a complement of 120 marines. The Carthaginian force was, however, larger, with 350 ships and 150,000 men. The two fleets met on a promontory of the southern coast of Sicily, Cape Ecnomus.

The Roman fleet assumed a triangle formation, with the *apex* towards the Carthaginians. The command galleys of the Roman *Consuls* – *Atilius Regulus* and *Manlius* – were two huge ships, each rowed by six banks of oars. Each side of the triangle formed a squadron; a third one, with the transport ships behind it, formed the base; a fourth squadron formed a reserve, ranged in one long line so as to cover both flanks of the squadrons before them.

The Carthaginians arranged their ships in open order, extending their line from the shore to sea with the intention of surrounding the Romans. Hamilcar was at the command of the left wing; the rest of the fleet was led by Hanno. The Romans began the attack. Seeing the weak line of single ships forming the Carthaginian centre, they bore down upon it. This was the plan of Hamilcar. He gave orders to his officers to retreat as soon as the attack began. The Romans eagerly pursued the flying enemy, breaking their order of battle, the two squadrons in advance being separated from the third and from the reserve. Suddenly the retreating Carthaginians turned upon their enemies. There followed a terrible fight, in which the Carthaginians tried to use their advantage in seamanship and in the speed of their ships, without daring to come to close quarters, to avoid the dreaded grappling and boarding machines of the Roman ships.

While this struggle was going on, Hanno bore down with his ships on the rear of the Roman fleet, attacking the reserve squadron and throwing it into confusion. The left or in-shore wing of the Carthaginian fleet attacked instead the squadron which protected the transports. But at close quarters the Carthaginians could not hold their own; Hamilcar retreated, and Hanno, who had been pressing hard on the transport squadron and the reserve, was attacked in his turn and forced to fly. This was the Romans' second great naval victory; they lost 26 ships, against 100 Carthaginian ships sunk and 64 captured with all their crews. Those that escaped were scattered in all directions, and Africa exposed to Roman attack.

The main problem of Carthage was that, when under attack in her own dominions, she was almost helpless. The invasion army found a rich and unarmed region. The Romans collected a rich booty, taking as many as 20,000 slaves. If instead of busying themselves with plunder they had advanced on Carthage at once, the war would probably have been finished at a single blow.

The hesitation of the Romans pushed the Senate to recall one part of the army in Italy. Regulus was left with 15,000 infantry and 600 horsemen, supported by 40 ships; the rest of the force, with the vast booty collected, was carried back to Italy. But even with only half of his forces, Regulus was able to win a brilliant victory, advancing and taking up a position at Tunes, only five miles from Carthage.

The situation of Carthage was desperate. Regulus, who was afraid that his year of consulship might expire before the war was finished, offered peace, but the terms were so harsh that the Carthaginians broke off the negotiation, resolving to resist to the last. Xanthippus, a Spartan commander, took command of the Carthaginian army and won a decisive battle in 255 BC. The *Consul* Regulus and 500 of his army were taken prisoners. Regulus, according to the tradition, after being kept in prison at Carthage for several years, was sent to Rome to negotiate a peace, under the promise to return if he failed. When brought into the Senate, he strongly advised his countrymen not to accept any conditions of peace, because Carthage was not able to fight for much longer. Then he returned to Carthage to face his terrible death.

After 20 years of ferocious war the naval battle of the Aegates Islands signed the definitive victory of the Romans. Carthage was in a difficult situation: the Romans were besieging Drepanon (nowadays Trapani), meanwhile the Punic galleys were inside the harbour of the city and their land army in Sicily. So the Carthaginians tried to rescue the elite army of Hamilcar by sending a fleet to the Aegates Islands, hiding them during the night and then embarking the army of Hamilcar, at the foot of the Eryx mountain. But the Romans, informed, waited for them: the general, Hanno, was defeated and his fleet destroyed. The admiral was crucified on his return to Carthage. The Senate of Carthage had no more finance for the war: in this same year 241 BC Carthage signed the treaty of peace with Rome. The conditions were very harsh: Carthage should abandon any pretension on Sicily and Sardinia, and pay an indemnity of 3,200 talents.

The Second Punic War
During the Second Punic War the Roman fleet was an essential instrument in the siege and conquest of Syracuse. Between 211 and 205 BC the Roman fleet participated in the war against Philip V of Macedonia with a fleet of at least 25 'Fives', and 35 *rostratae* which were brought with the army to

Silver *denarius* of Gnaeus Pompeius Magnus, Proconsol. On the verso, a *prora rostrata* of a Roman warship, celebrating the victorious war against the Cilician pirates. (Roma, Medagliere Capitolino, photo D. Carro, courtesy of Musei Capitolini, Roma)

Dyrrachion from Publius Sempronius. Apart from the wars against Philip, the Roman fleet was the protagonist of important activities: the *Consul* Marcellus (Livy, XXIV,36–46) laid siege to Syracuse and blockaded the city with his fleet in 217 BC, making use of towers mounted on 'Fives' in linked pairs. According Silius Italicus, during the naval battle against the Carthaginian fleet in front of the city, a Punic 'Seven' was set on fire by a tower mounted on two 'Threes'. In 208 BC, expecting a Carthaginian attack on the coasts of Italy, the Senate formed a powerful fleet of 100 warships: 50 ships were sent to Scipio from Spain, and to the Sicilian squadron of 70 vessels another 30 were added from Rome's Tarentine allies. To defend the coast near Rome, the Urban *Praetor* refitted 30 old ships in Ostia, and added to this 20 warships from the *socii navales*. In the summer the Sicilian fleet of 100 ships raided the coasts of Africa and routed a Carthaginian fleet of 83 ships near Clupea (Aspis). But the main exploit of the Roman navy, after a further naval action in the waters of Gibraltar, was the ferrying to Africa of the army of Scipio, who won the decisive battle of Zama in 202 BC. This involved a convoy of 400 transport ships escorted by two squadrons of warships, each 20 *rostratae*-strong.

Rome's victory in the Punic Wars opened the way for its hegemony in the Mediterranean Sea: after Carthage, the main enemies of Rome on land and sea were the powerful Hellenic kingdoms of Syria and Macedonia.

Relief from Narbonne, showing a Caesarian ship in battle with armed crew, second quarter of 1st century BC. (Narbonne, Lapidarium, author's photo)

Operations in Greece
In 198 BC the Roman fleet operating in Greece and that of her allies was comprised of 100 *cataphractae* (*naves tectae*), of which 56 were Roman, and 30 *lemboi*. The Roman fleet was probably formed by three *quinqueremes*, while the other *longae naves* were mainly *quadriremes* and *triremes*. The military operations against the Syrians were conducted by the *Consul* Livius, with a fleet of 81 *cataphractae* and many smaller ships – *aphracts* fitted with rams, and *navigia speculatoria*. Flagships were usually 'Sixes' at that time, or larger *polyremes*. These ships and those of their Rhodian allies allowed the Romans to obtain a striking success at the final battle of Myonnesos, in 190 BC, over the fleet of Antiochos the Great.

G

CAESAR'S SHIPS IN ARMORICA, 56 BC
The scene shows two of Caesar's ships in action against two Venetian ships in the Morbihan. The Venetians possessed square sailboats, 30–40m long and 10–12m wide, without oars. They were very high on the water, so the crews were protected against the Roman missiles. During the naval battle which took place at Lorient, with the fleet of Caesar fighting against 220 Venetian ships, the Romans managed to recover their initial disadvantage by cutting the halyards of their opponents with sharp hooks inserted in, and nailed to, long poles (*dorydrepania*); the leather sails fell, thus immobilizing the Veneti and allowing the Romans to board. The main ship is a Roman *liburna*, copied from the Aquileia Doric Frieze commemorating the Legion of Caesar participating in the campaign. The ship half-visible on the left is copied from the 'Five' of the Ostia relief, and shows her rowing system.

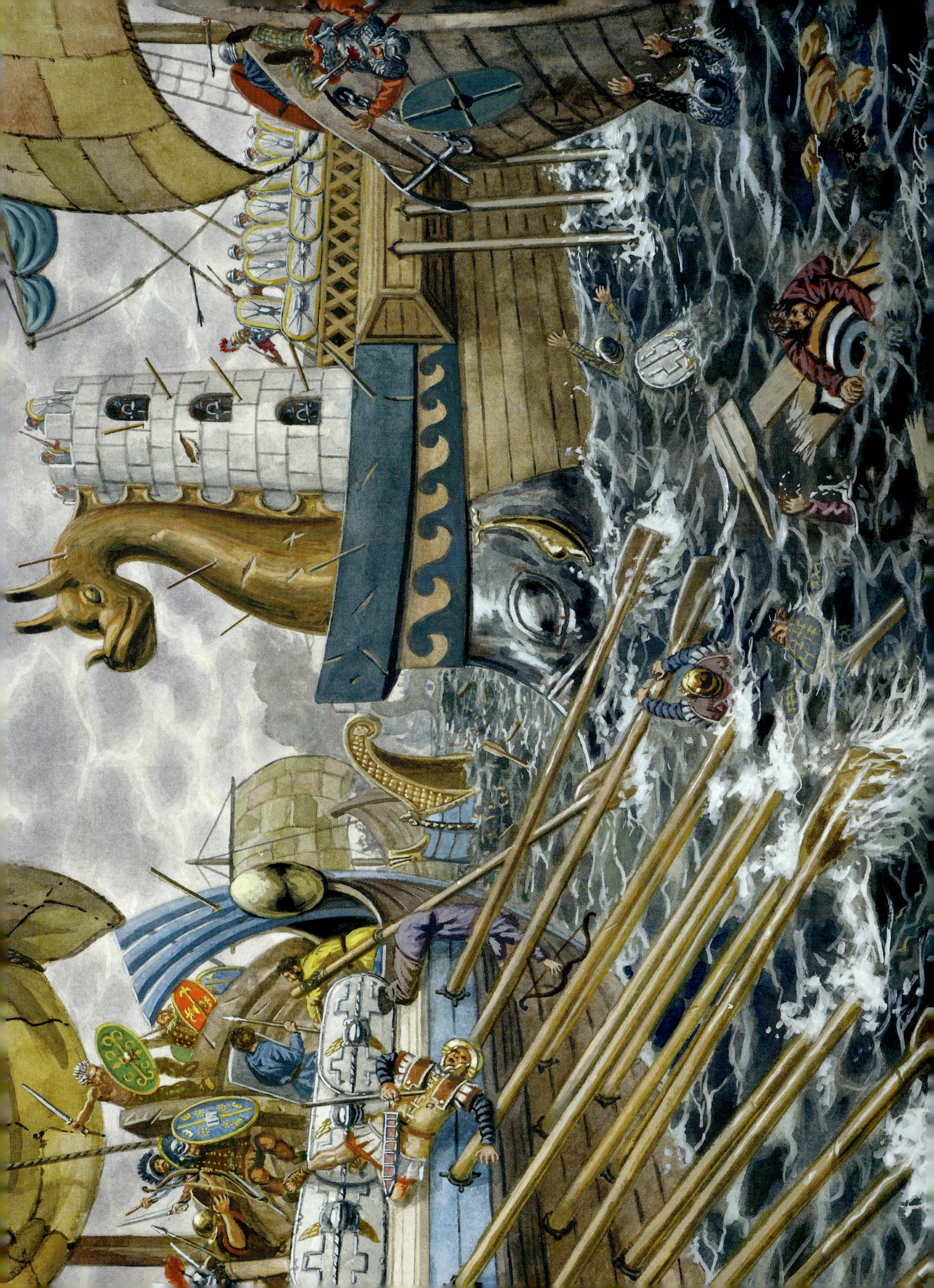

Faro of Messina and warship, represented on coins minted by Sextus Pompeius. On the lighthouse there is a statue of Neptune with trident; below, a naval unit. (Silver denarius preserved in the Medagliere Capitolino, photo D. Carro, courtesy of the museum)

Funerary monument of the 1st century BC or 1st century AD from the cimitero dei Giordani, Rome, showing a liburna with his armed crew in action. (Rome, Museum of the Civiltà Romana, cast, author's photo)

Pompey and the Cilician Pirates

The most extraordinary naval effort of the Roman republic in the first half of the 1st century BC was the expedition of Pompey the Great against the Cilician pirates, conducted with 500 ships and *hemioliai cataphractae*. In the civil war against Caesar the same Pompey collected 500 warships and a vast number of *liburnides* and *kataskopoi*: 'In the meantime a great force was gathered by Pompey. His navy was simply irresistible, since he had 500 fighting ships (*machimoi*), while the number of his scout ships (*kataskopoi*) and fast cruisers (*liburnides*) was immense' (Plutarch, *Pompey*, 64,1). Combined passages from Plutarch, Livy and Appian allow us to say that in the Roman fleets of the 2nd and 1st centuries BC they employed *cataphract* ships with rams, *aphracts* with rams, ramless oared ships (*lemboi*), and *pristis*, i.e. *lemboi* fitted with rams. Some of them performed the duty of scout ships (*navigia exploratoria, kataskopoi*).

Caesar in Gaul

Interested in the wealth of the northern islands, Julius Caesar – who had studied the writings on these places with accuracy – risked taking a Roman fleet into the Atlantic. He first encountered the Veneti Armoricani, who were considered the best naval warriors of the Celtic tribes of the Atlantic coast. These proud sailors of Brittany were part of the Celtic confederation of the North Sea, including the Bretons of Great Britain, which ruled over the tin trade of Sorlingues, the gold of southwest Great Britain, the Baltic amber and other products sought by the Mediterranean market. In the summer of 56 BC, they threw off the Roman yoke, taking Caesar's ambassadors hostage. The Veneti inhabited the islands of the Morbihan coast, attached to the mainland at low tide, isolated by the ocean at high tide. No fortress was ever so moated, discouraging any siege. When the stubborn Romans had success, however, in penetrating their ramparts, the Veneti embarked families and property, and took refuge in a friendly city. Caesar then decided to confront their strong fleet of about 220 cargo ships, which could be turned into heavy warships.

The most astonishing naval victory which Caesar won in Gaul was the battle of the bay of Qiberon. Caesar (*DBG*, III,8–10) requisitioned merchant ships from the allied Celtic peoples and ordered them to build warships (*longae naves*) on the river Loire, raising Celtic rowers (*remiges*) from the Roman Provincia, (nowadays Provence) and providing sailors (*nautae*) and steermen (*gubernatores*). We have no description of the ships built, but presumably they were *triremes*, *quinqueremes* and *liburnians*.

The Venetian boats, with their flat bottoms, easily moved among weather shoals and ebb-tide, in contrast to the Roman ships. With their leather sails and iron anchors suspended on chains, these Celtic ships were designed for the Atlantic squalls. Three times higher above the sea than the Romans' hastily built *liburnians*, their thick hulls were proof against Roman rams, and it was difficult for the legionaries to reach those who overwhelmed them with missiles from above. The Veneti had no difficulty in adjusting their shots to harass them. Limited to a few shooters, assault towers set on *liburnians* did not compensate for the power of enemy shooting. The only advantage of the Romans lay in the human engine of their rowers, which allowed them to move freely; the Veneti were instead dependent on the wind. With scythed weapons attached to the end of long shafts, the Romans, commanded by Decimus Brutus – future murderer of Caesar – slashed the enemy sails or cut their shrouds, managing to stop the enemy fleet and attacked each Venetian vessel more than once, eventually overwhelming them. Caesar then massacred their entire aristocracy and sold the population in slavery.

The naval wars of Octavianus and Agrippa

At the beginning of the last civil wars of the Roman Republic the Mediterranean shores were only partially under the control of Rome, while the waters were out of her control. After the defeat of Brutus and Cassius, in fact, most of the remains of their powerful fleets eventually flocked to the command of Sextus Pompeius, son of the great Pompeius, whom the Senate had improvidently given the command of all naval forces, not imagining that he could devote himself to piracy *pro domo sua*.

Octavian, 19 years old at Caesar's death, was not only the legal but also the spiritual heir of the greatest of the Romans, and assumed the protection of Italy and the West. But for strategic genius, the most gifted was his admiral, Marcus Vipsanius Agrippa, who was also particularly attentive to battlefield geography. For the reconstruction of their naval campaigns we must first rely on ancient literature, including poetry. Other writings of interest have been added in recent years thanks to the analysis of Egyptian papyri, while new elements have been drawn from the epigraphic and numismatic sources.

The naval power of Sextus, who had arbitrarily established himself in Sicily and had trusted the command of his fleets to former pirate chieftains captured by his father, was a cause of serious alarm for Octavian, since Italy, under his jurisdiction, was increasingly starved by pirate attacks against

Scene of naval battle, possibly Actium, with marines embarked on a *liburna* and a detail of the ram. (Isernia, Museo Archeologico, photo D. Carro, courtesy of the museum)

39

Prow of the Arch of Orange ships, 14 BC or 21 AD. The ships of the Orange Arch are those of the Frejus Fleet, and they represent the captured Cleopatra's fleet. Interestingly, no foredeck is provided. (Drawing by Andrea Salimbeti ex Morrison and Coates)

merchant shipping and along its coasts. During the absence of Agrippa – who was governor of Gaul for two years – Octavian had faced Sextus with two fleets, earning two brief successes (Cumae and Cape Pelorus) and finally suffering very considerable losses directly caused by bad weather. Sextus Pompey thanked Neptune and declared himself the son of the god, whose blue robe he wore. But at the end of that year Marcus Agrippa returned to Italy to take his first consulship (37 BC) and the command of the war at sea.

When Agrippa received the command of Octavian's fleet for the final engagement against Sextus, to escape the raids of Sextus's fleet on the coastal shipyards he assembled and fitted out his ships in the newly created base on the Lucrine Lake. The young commander in chief, not yet 26 years old, looked from the beginning for the most ambitious target of naval strategy: complete command of the sea. His first goal was not to meet and defeat Sextus's fleets of pirates in naval battle, but to wipe out any threat from the Tyrrhenian Sea. Therefore, although Octavian had already acquired a number of shipyards and would successfully ask Marcus Antonius for another 120 vessels in exchange for legionaries, Agrippa designed and created a new navy, with all the necessary components: shipyards, military ports, naval bases, training centres, housing, logistics and security systems. He also oversaw the recruitment of staff and the design of more robust and better-armed ships. Agrippa conceived engagements in which his ships, higher and larger than those of his enemy, would allow their deck soldiers to prevail over those of Sextus: so he ensured that many ships were *cataphractae*, i.e. with good protection for the oarsmen. He also paid special attention to training the new crews on shore and at sea, exploiting the days of bad weather to accustom men to navigation in the most arduous conditions.

H

ROMAN *LIBURNA*, 31 BC

Reconstruction of a Liburnian ship of Agrippa from the relief of Isernia. The *liburnae* appear to have been decked and boxed in. They were smaller and faster ships, armed with 82 oars dispersed in two orders, about 108ft long, with 114 oarsmen, 10–15 sailors and 40 marines. The hull design of the *liburna* shows a pointed, streamlined prow, clearly built for speed. Ancient authors recognised the streamlining of the bodies of birds and *liburnians* as analogous and designed for the same end. According to Appian (*Rom. Hist*. X,1,3) the Romans called the light and pointed (*oksea*) ships of the Illyrians with two oar levels (*dikrota*) liburnians. The ram which the word pointed suggests confirms the epithet of Propertius (*Odes*, IV,11.44) as *rostrata* and the presence of an armament to be used as occasion might demand for defence or offence.

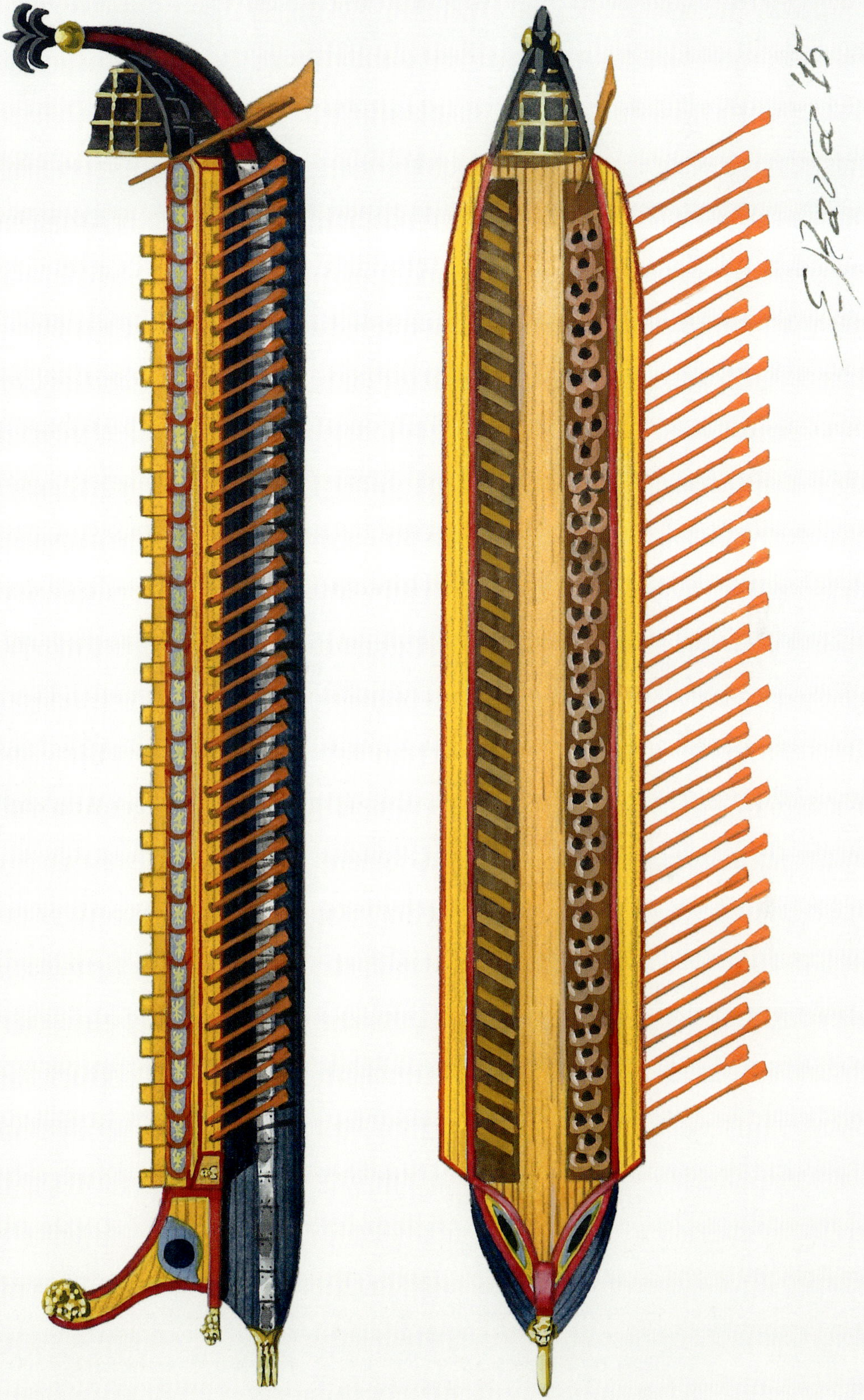

Details of ships from the Arch of Orange, 14 BC or 21 AD. (in situ, Orange, France, author's photo)

In the spring of 36 BC, the powerful new naval force was ready for combat. The plan of Agrippa, approved by Octavian, was to bring together three fleets to invest Sicily at the same time from the three seas: the African fleet with the legions of Lepidus would attack from the Strait of Sicily; the Ionian fleet of Octavian from Taranto (with the ships of Marcus Antonius), which should also land the legions available in Italy; and Agrippa's fleet from his bases.

Despite bad weather, the plan fully attained the desired result: Sextus Pompeius, finding himself stuck in the north-east tip of the island with food supplies cut from both land and sea, was forced to take his fleet into action against that of Agrippa, and he was defeated in the waters of Naulocus, losing all his ships except the 17 with which he fled (to later face his death). His maritime power had been destroyed and the Tyrrhenian Sea was once again safe.

Octavian's focus moved now logically to the other side of Italy, as the Adriatic coasts and their commercial traffic was the target of repeated hostile actions by the endemic Illyrian pirates nestled between the coast and the islands of Dalmatia. In the spring of 35 BC, Octavian launched the war against them; while this war lasted two years, the available sources have reported only a few details: in addition to Octavian (who was wounded), Agrippa also fought here. The Roman fleet annihilated the hideouts of pirates existing in the islands of Mljet (Meleda) and Korcula (Curzola), then reached the region of Kvarner (Quarnaro), where the Romans seized all the ships of the Liburni pirates and Segna, their capital. The same fleet, which allegedly used the ports of Ancona, Ravenna, Senj (Segna), Zadar (Zara) and Solin (Salona), also contributed to the conquest of Metulo, capital of Giapidi, and to support the forces operating in the hinterland. The following year the fleet made a decisive contribution to the blockade of food supplies to the Dalmatian rebels, who surrendered finally, in the winter of 34–33 BC, exhausted by privation. With this war Agrippa extended the dominion of Octavianus on the whole Adriatic Sea, introducing to the Roman fleet further fast *liburnae* and providing a valuable lesson on the strategic use of naval power.

After the naval victory of Agrippa at Naulocus, the successful removal of the *triumvir* Lepidus had left only Octavian and Antony ruling Rome. The dream of a revival of the eastern empire of Alexander the Great under the aegis of a Hellenistic ruler clearly contributed to the success of the call to arms of Antony and Cleopatra, who managed with several Eastern kings to form a broad coalition against Rome. At Ephesus a huge naval force was assembled, consisting of 700 warships (including 200 of Cleopatra's own) and 300 *onerariae*. In spring 32 BC the ships sailed to Samos and Alene. From there the naval force set sail in the autumn and went into the Ionian Sea. After having posted some ships to protect the ports in Greece, the fleet went to the Strait of Otranto, towards Italy.

We cannot be certain if the couple had actually intention to land immediately in Italy to take Octavian by surprise, as reported by Cassius Dio (50.9). He states that they stopped course at Corfu, there being vessels (obviously of Agrippa) on patrol in the Strait of Otranto. Then they reversed the course and decided to spend the winter with the ships at Actium.

Agrippa's strategy was to blockade the enemy's ports in the Gulf of Ambracia systematically and relentlessly, severing all their lines of supply, in order to ensure that this would be the terminal point of the expedition and realize the dreams of the Eastern coalition. Once the weather made it possible (probably by March 31) he took his fleet into the Ionian Sea, using Comaro Bay (adjacent to Actium, but poorly protected in case of storms) as an advance naval base. In addition to controlling the mouth of the Gulf of Ambracia, he worked even more to the south and intercepted all commercial traffic carrying food and weapons from Egypt and Syria. Using surprise naval raids he gradually took possession of all the key points manned by naval and land forces of the Eastern coalition: Meton, defended by the deposed king of Mauretania, Bogud, and the optimal base for the control of traffic in the Ionian Sea; Corfu, possession of which allowed Octavian to safely transfer

Rostrum of Roman ship from Acqualadroni, during its recovery, decorated in the shape of the Neptunus Trident, 36 BC. The bronze piece, found in Acqualadroni, Messina, is perhaps related to the fleet of Sextus Pompeius; rams shaped like tridents were a constant in the Roman navy, visible also on the coins of the *Fonteia Gens*. (Photo courtesy of the Soprintendenza del Mare della Regione Siciliana)

BELOW
Detail of the back part of the previous ram, still with part of the wood inserted, 36 BC. (Photo courtesy of the Soprintendenza del Mare della Regione Siciliana)

BELOW LEFT
Detail of the trident's blades of the previous ram, 36 BC. (Photo courtesy of the Soprintendenza del Mare della Regione Siciliana)

Roman warship, with closed sail, represented fighting nearby the shore. The fresco, probably representing a scene of the Illyrian Wars, was found in the villa where Agrippa lived with his wife, the young daughter of Augustus, Julia. (Fresco of Villa of Farnesina, Roma, Museo Nazionale Romano, photo D. Carro, courtesy of the museum)

the fleet with the legions from Brindisi to Epirus; the island of Lefkada, which provided a more protected anchorage in front of Actium; and Patras and Corinth, to deprive the enemy of any remaining chance of receiving food from the east.

At the same time he twice defeated in battle the enemy naval formations. The first was deployed in defence of Patras and at the entrance to the Gulf of Corinth; the second was the only one which tried to breach the naval blockade. The defeat of the latter, in the second half of August, further depressed the morale of the forces of the Eastern coalition, already decimated by hunger and disease, and caused constant desertions and increasing defections of persons of high rank.

The situation had deteriorated to such an extent that Antony and Cleopatra were forced to sail, hoping to defeat Octavian at sea, or at least to save what could be saved for a possible counterattack. Having armed ships with the best men and set fire to the remaining units, they finally came to Actium where the

Another naval scene from the fresco of the Villa of Farnesina. (Roma, Museo Nazionale Romano, photo D. Carro, courtesy of the museum)

whole naval force of Octavian was getting ready, commanded by Agrippa and made up of veterans of the previous two naval wars, with the addition of small and fast *liburnians*. The Eastern fleet was less numerous, but included a large number of Phoenician and Egyptian *polyremes*, which compensated for the lack of manoeuvrability with superior skills for offence and defence. Agrippa broadly had the edge in terms of crew quality.

In the final confrontation between Octavian and Agrippa and the fleets of Antony and Cleopatra, most of the Roman fleet was composed of *liburnians*, which harassed the largest Ptolemaic *polyremes*. The tactical performance of the battle can be reconstructed with reasonable reliability. It began with a long wait, in which each of the two fleets, both well-positioned to face each other, waited for the first movement of the other to derive immediate benefit. Then the usual sea breeze started, which began from the west-south-west and progressively rotated until it became a Mistral (northwesterly), gradually bracing.

The first movement was carried forward from the Eastern ships, perhaps to compensate for the effect of the wind. It provoked an immediate reaction from the Roman fleet: the right wing of it, under the command of Octavian, manoeuvred to outflank the enemy to the south, while the left side, commanded by Agrippa, was extended considerably to the north-east, rowing swiftly against the sea and the wind to disrupt and surround from the north Antony's formation. The early engagements began, being excessively difficult for the Romans while the enemy formation remained firm. The above-mentioned operation was followed by the phase of naval attacks (with thrown weapons and bolts) and boardings, a phase in which the better training and better morale of the crews of Agrippa achieved greater success.

At this point, Cleopatra, whose squadron of 60 ships was in a protected position from the rest of the fleet, ordered her ships to raise their sails, and taking advantage of the gap formed at the centre of both sides, went with the wind in her sails to the south-east, soon followed by Antony – embarked on a *quinquereme* – and perhaps some other unit of the latter. The fugitives were immediately chased by fast *liburnians*, which managed to reach the rowing *quinquereme* of Antony, but then had to give up, unable to compete with the increasing wind. The other ships of the Eastern fleet continued to fight stubbornly, despite calls to lay down their arms, and the battle continued to rage, with the Romans finding it difficult to board the *polyremes* which had much higher sides than those of the assailants' ships. Agrippa resorted to the solution he had already prepared, foreseeing the possibility of a situation like this: the massive use of firing projectiles on the naval units that had not yet been boarded. The naval victory was achieved at dusk and it turned out to be decisive; the next morning, at least 140 ships had been captured or destroyed, and the command of the sea was now firmly in the hands of those who had proved themselves more worthy. Although Antony and Cleopatra had fled to Egypt with between 60 and 90 ships, their dreams and the entire coalition were irretrievably wrecked in the waters east of Actium. The Roman naval forces, created and commanded by Agrippa, had no rivals.

The next year, to attack Alexandria from the sea and from both sides of the Egyptian coast, Octavian detached Cornelius Gallus with a fleet to Cyrenaica, while the young Caesar, with his own fleet, sailed along the eastern shore of the Mediterranean. The spontaneous disappearance of the

Alexandrian fleet at the arrival of Octavian caused the suicide of Antony, followed some time later by that of Cleopatra, and the annexation of Egypt to the Roman Empire. Leaving Alexandria after only one month, Octavian left intact the fleet of Cleopatra, took it under his direct command and subsequently named it *Classis Augusta Alexandrina*.

The victory was celebrated throughout the Empire with great emphasis. In addition to the traditional honours and triumphs in Rome, to jubilation throughout the Empire – even in Alexandria – the celebrations included the establishment of the four-year games known as *Aziadi*, a naval show with eight ships of the Eastern fleet, the foundation of Nicopolis (city of the victory) and the dedication of the monument to the battle.

SELECT BIBLIOGRAPHY

Ancient Roman sources
(I used mainly the Loeb translations and texts, if not otherwise specified):
Appian, *Mithridatic War; Civil Wars*
Caesar, *De Bello Gallico* (DBG)
Cassius Dio, *Roman History*
Cicero, *Verrines; Ad Atticum*
Ennius, *Framenta*
Florus, *Epitome of Roman History*
Frontinus, *Stratagemata*
Hirtius, *De Bello Alexandrino* (HBA)
Horatius, *Odes and Epodes*
Incerti autoris, *Celeuma* in *The Hundred Best Poems (lyrical) in the Latin Language*, J.V. Mackail (ed.), London, 1906
Livy, *History of Rome from the Founding of the City*
Lucan, *De Bello Civilis sive Pharsalia*
Ovidius, *Metamorphosis*
Plautus, *Poenulus; Mercator*
Pliny the Elder, *Historia Naturalis*
Polybius, *Roman History*
Plutarch, *Parallel Lives* (Antonius, Cato the Younger, Pompeius Magnus)
Propertius, *Odes*
Sallust, *Roman History*
Silius Italicus, *Punica*
Valerius Maximus, *Memorable Deeds and Sayings*
Vergilius, *Aeneid*
Vitruvius, *De Architectura*

Modern works
Abranson, E., and Colbus, J.P., *La vita dei Legionari ai tempi della guerra in Gallia*, Milano, 1979
Carro, D., 'Le origini', in *Classica, Storia della marina di Roma, Testimonianze dell'antichità*, nr. I, Roma, 1992
Carro, D., 'Le grandi coalizioni marittime nell'arcipelago', in *Classica, Storia della marina di Roma, Testimonianze dell'antichità*, nr. I, Roma, 1994
Carro, D., 'Pompeo Magno e il dominio del mare', in *Classica, Storia della marina di Roma, Testimonianze dell'antichità*, nr. VI, Roma, 1997

Carro, D., 'Vessillo Azzurro, la strategia navale di Agrippa in tre guerre marittime e per la pace augustea', in *Naval History*, 2014, 121–44

Cowan, R., *Roman Legionary, 58 BC–AD 69*, Oxford, 2003

D'Amato, R., *Imperial Roman Naval Forces 31 BC–AD 500*, Oxford, 2009

D'Amato, R., *Arms and Armour of the Imperial Roman Soldier, from Marius to Commodus 112 BC–AD 192*, London, 2009

Daremberg, C.V., and Saglio, E., *Dictionnaire des Antiquités Grecques et Romaines*, Paris, 1877–1919

Eckstein, A.N., *Senate and General: Individual Decision-making and Roman Foreign Relations, 264–194BC*, Los Angeles, 1987

Fede Berti, *Fortuna Maris, la nave romana di Comacchio*, Bologna, 1990

Henniquiau, M., and Martin, J., *La Marine Antique (2)*, Pantin, 1999

Lazenby, J.F., *The first Punic War: A Military History*, London, 1996

Liberati, A.M., 'Navigare con gli antichi', *Archeo 8 (1997)*, 45–93

Liberati, A.M., Silverio, E. and Silverio F., 'L'esercito e la marina militare nell'antica Roma', in *Roma Archeologica*, 18–19, July 2003

Ministero per i beni culturali ed ambientali, *Aquileia, Basilika, Museen und Ausgrabungen*, Roma, 1996

Morrison, J. S., and Gardiner, R., (eds.), *The Age of the Galley: Mediterranean Oared Vessels Since Pre-Classical Time*, Conway Maritime, London, 1995

Morrison, J. S., and Coates, J.F., *Greek and Roman Oared Warships*, Oxford, 1996

Mueller, H.F., *Roman Religion in Valerius Maximus*, London & New York, 2002

Murray, W.W., *The Age of Titans, Rise and Fall of the Great Hellenistic Navies*, Oxford, 2013

Pitassi, M., *The Navies of Rome*, Chippenham and Eastbourne, 2009

Santa Maria Scrinari, V., *Sculture Romane di Aquileia*, Roma, 1972

Sekunda, N., *Republican Roman Army, 200–104 BC*, London, 1996

Various, *Genti nel Delta, Uomini, territori e culto dall'antichità all'alto Medioevo*, Ferrara, 2007

Venturoli, P. (ed.), *Arma virumque cano, le armi preistoriche e classiche dell'armeria reale di Torino*, Torino, 2002

Walker, S,. and Higgs, P., *Cleopatra regina d'Egitto*, Milano, 2000

Warry, J., *Warfare in the Classical World*, London, 1980

INDEX

Page numbers in **bold** refer to illustrations and their captions.

Actium, battle of 14, 16, **18**, 23, **39**, 44–45
actuariae 19
Aegates, battle of 22, **22**, 23, **F(32, 33)**, **34**, 35
Agrippa, Marcus Vipsanius 11, 23, 24, 39–40, 42, 43–45, **44**
Aineias 4
Alba Fucentia graffito **14**
Alexander of Epirus 7
Alexandria 45–46
anchors 9, **34**
Ancus Marcius, King 5
Antiates, the 7
Antikythera mechanism, the 22
Antikythera shipwreck 10
Antiochos the Great 14
Antium 7
aphractae 4, 12, 31
apotropaic eyes 9, 11, 15, **15**, 20
Appian 38, **H(40, 41)**
Appius Claudius 31
Aristhonos 10
Aristodemus, 5
Athens 5
Augustus 16

Bellum Aziacum, the 16
Benoit. Fernand 10
block **19**
boarding actions 23–24, 26, **F(32, 33)**
Bruttium 7
Brutus, Decimus 18, 39

Caesar, Julius **G(36, 37)**, 38–39
Caius Duilius 23, 32
Caius Menius 7
Camillus, Lucius Furius 6, 7
Camillus, Marcus Furius 6
Campania 10
Carthage 4, 9, 23. *see also* Punic Wars
  sea treaties 5, 6–7, 8
Cassius Dio 43
cataphractae 11, 14, 18, 22, 36, 40
Cato the Younger 14
Cicero 14
Cilician pirates, defeat of **C(20, 21)**, 35, 38
Civil War 38
Cleopatra 42–46
colour 20
Comacchio ship, the 22
construction techniques 9–10
Consular Age, the 5
corvus, the 4, 23–24, 32, **F(32, 33)**
Cuma 5

decks 10, 12, **A1(12, 13)**
decoration 18, **20**, 20, 22, **32**
  rams **22**, **23**, **26**, **27**
Delphi 6
Diekplous, the 27
dimensions 10, **B1(16, 17)**
Drepanon, siege of 35

equipment 22
  sailors 5, **28**

Farnesina frescos **44**
Faro of Messina 38

flagships 15–16, 36
formations 34

Gaul 38–39
Greece 6, 36

Hamilcar 34–35
Hannibal 32, 34
Hanno 34–35
harpax, the 24
hemioliai cataphract 14, 38
hemiolia-triimiolia **D1(24, 25)**
hulls, iron-reinforced wood 9

Isola Tiberina, the 9

kataskopoi 14, 19
Korykos, battle of 14

ladders 22, **E(28, 29)**
Latium 4, 6
legionaries 24, **F(32, 33)**
lembos biremes 12, **A2(12, 13)**, 18
liburnae 14, 18, 19, **G(36, 37)**, 38, **H(40, 41)**, 45
Lipara, battle of 32
Livius 36
Livy 5, 8, 11, 12, 14, **E(28, 29)**, 38
Lucan 18

Marcellus **E(28, 29)**, 36
marines 12, 18, 24, 34, 39
Mark Antony 22–23, 40, 42–46
Merlin, Alfred 10
Mylae, battle of 32
myoparones 19

nails 10
name-devices 9, 22
Narbonne relief **36**
Naulocos, battle of 24, 42
naves actuariae 19

oar panels 10
oar strokes 28
oarboxes 11, **11**, **A1(12, 13)**, 15, **D2(24, 25)**
oars 16, 19, **D2(24, 25)**, 26
oarsmen 14, 14–15, **B1(16, 17)**
  disposition 27–28, 30
  rhythm 28, 30, **31**
Octavian 39–40, 42–46
Odysseus 5, 7
onerariae cargo ships 10, 19
Orange Arch, the 20, 22, **40**, 42
Ostia 5, 15
outriggers 16
Ovidius 20

Palazzo Barberini Mosaic 12
patera 10, **11**
penteconterae 10, 12
Periplous, the 27
Philip V of Macedonia 35–36
pirates 18, **C(20, 21)**
Plutarch 11, 19, 38
Polybius 5, 6, 9, 24, **E(28, 29)**, 32
polyremes 15–16, **16**, 18
Pompeii 8
Pompey the Great 18, **C(20, 21)**, **D(24, 25)**, 38
proembolion 9, 15, **15**, 18, 20, **20**, 22

prow ornaments 10
Publius Cornelius 8
Punic Wars 7, 20, 23
  First 4, 9–10, 15, 31–32, **F(32, 33)**, 34–35, **34**
  Second 35–36

Qiberon, battle of 38–39
quadriremes 14, **14**, 31
quinqueremes 10, **10**, **A1(12, 13)**, 14–15, **15**, **B2(16, 17)**, 24, **D2(24, 25)**, 31, 32, 36
  rower disposition 28, 30, **F(32, 33)**
  sieges **E(28, 29)**

rams 9, 11, **A1(12, 13)**, 15, 22, 22–23, 23, **D(24, 25)**, 26, 27, 39, **H(40, 41)**, **43**
raven, the (*corvus*) 4, 23–24, 32, **F(32, 33)**
Regulus 35
Roman navy
  first mention 5–6
  origins 4–5, 31–32
  rise of 7–9
Romulus and Remus 4
rostratae 11
rowing
  disposition 27–28, 30, **F(32, 33)**
  rhythm 28, 30

sailors, equipment 5, **28**
sails **B2(16, 17)**
Sallust 19
Samnite wars 7–8
Sardinia 7, 34
scaphae 19
Scipio, Gnaeus Cornelius 31–32
scout ships 18, 19
Sextus Pompeius 23, 24, 39–40, 42
shields 11, 18
shipwrights 10
Sicily 7, 31
sieges 15, 19, **E(28, 29)**, 35–36
Silius Italicus 15, **E(28, 29)**, 36
stemposts 12, 15, 18
sternposts 11, **A1(12, 13)**, 15, 34
Strait of Messina 31–32
streamlining **H(40, 41)**
structure 10–11
Syracuse, siege of 15, 19, **E(28, 29)**, 35–36

tactics 11, 26–27, 32
Tarentine, the 6
Tarentum 8
Tarquin the Proud 5
Tiber, river 5
towers and turrets 8, 18, 24, 27, 39
triimiolia 12
triremes 8–9, 10, **10**, 14, **B1(16, 17)**
  rower disposition 27–28, 30

Vatican relief 18
Veii 5
Veneti Armoricani, the **G(36, 37)**, 38–39
Virgil 14
Vitruvius 27

war machines 24
warships 11
winged victories 22
wood 10